Gender

and

Discourse

ALSO BY DEBORAH TANNEN

Framing in Discourse (edited, 1993)

Gender and Conversational Interaction (edited, 1993)

You Just Don't Understand: Women and Men in Conversation (1990)

Talking Voices: Repetition, Dialogue and Imagery in Conversational Discourse (1989)

Linguistics in Context: Connecting Observation and Understanding (edited, 1988)

That's Not What I Meant! How Conversational Style Makes or Breaks Your Relations with Others (1986)

Languages and Linguistics: The Interdependence of Theory, Data and Application (coedited with James E. Alatis, 1986)

Perspectives on Silence (coedited with Muriel Saville-Troike, 1985)

Conversational Style: Analyzing Talk Among Friends (1984)

Coherence in Spoken and Written Discourse (edited, 1984)

Lilika Nakos (1983)

Spoken and Written Language: Exploring Orality and Literacy (edited, 1982)

Analyzing Discourse: Text and Talk (edited, 1982)

Gender

and

Discourse

Deborah Tannen

New York   Oxford

OXFORD UNIVERSITY PRESS

1994

Oxford University Press

Oxford   New York   Toronto
Delhi   Bombay   Calcutta   Madras   Karachi
Kuala Lumpur   Singapore   Hong Kong   Tokyo
Nairobi   Dar es Salaam   Cape Town
Melbourne   Auckland   Madrid

and associated companies in
Berlin   Ibadan

Copyright © 1994 by Deborah Tannen

Published by Oxford University Press, Inc.
200 Madison Avenue, New York, New York 10016

Oxford is a registered trademark of Oxford University Press, Inc.

Library of Congress Cataloging-in-Publication Data
Tannen, Deborah.
Gender and discourse / Deborah Tannen.
p. cm.   Includes bibliographical references and index.
ISBN 0–19–508975–8
1. Language and languages—Sex differences.
2. Discourse analysis. 3. Conversation. I. Title.
P120.S48T36   1994
401'.41—dc20   93–38839

Chapter 4 originally appeared in the journal *Semiotica* (1984) and is reprinted with
permission from Mouton de Gruyter, a division of Walter de Gruyter & Co.

Permission to reprint selections from the following is gratefully acknowledged:

Scenes from a Marriage by Ingmar Bergman, translated by Alan Blair. English
translation copyright © 1974 by Alan Blair. Reprinted by permission of
Pantheon Books, a division of Random House, Inc.

Mountain Language by Harold Pinter, copyright © 1988 by Harold Pinter.
Used with the permission of Grove/Atlantic Monthly Press.

Fear of Flying by Erica Jong, copyright © 1973 by Erica Jong. Reprinted by
permission of Henry Holt Co.

Like Life by Lorrie Moore, copyright © 1990 by Lorrie Moore. Reprinted by
permission of Alfred A. Knopf, Inc.

4 6 8 9 7 5 3

Printed in the United States of America
on acid-free paper

*To Barbara McGrael
and in memory of
Larry McGrael*

Acknowledgments

I prepared this book for publication while a fellow at the Center for Advanced Study in the Behavioral Sciences in Stanford, California. I shall always be grateful to have been a part of the Center for a year. I am also grateful for financial support provided through CASBS by the National Science Foundation SES–9022192.

Contents

Contents

Contents

Gender
and
Discourse

Introduction

ENTERING THE ARENA of research on gender is like step-
ping into a maelstrom. What it means to be female or male,
what it's like to talk to someone of the other (or the same) gender,
are questions whose answers touch people where they live, and
when a nerve is touched, people howl. Yet it is my hope that
through the din, scholarly research can be heard, and dialogue can
take place among researchers, even those who have entered the
room of scholarly exchange through different disciplinary doors.

One of the aspects of gender studies that makes it most reward-
ing and meaningful is also one that makes it especially risky: its
interdisciplinary nature. When scholars from different fields try to
read and comment on each other's research, they find themselves
on dangerous ground. Interdisciplinary dialogue is in itself a kind of
cross-cultural communication, because researchers bring with them
completely different notions of what questions to ask and how to go
about answering them.[1] Assumptions that are taken for granted by
those in one discipline are often deemed groundless by those in
another. For example, psychologists trained in experimental
methods may scorn and discount ethnographic or hermeneutic
studies because they lack large data bases, random sampling, control groups, and statistical analysis. And anthropologists trained in

ethnographic methods may scorn and discount psychological studies because they are based on data elicited in experimental rather than naturally occurring situations and reduce the complex texture of human behavior to quantifiable and "codable" abstractions.

The study of gender and language might seem at first to be a narrowly focused field, but it is actually as interdisciplinary as they come. Researchers working in this area have their roots in wildly divergent academic disciplines, including sociology, education, anthropology, psychology, speech communication, literature, and women's studies, as well as my own field of linguistics. Though one might expect scholars trained in linguistics—the academic discipline devoted to the study of language—to figure prominently in this group, linguists are in fact the smallest contingent. I suspect this is mostly because the field is very small to start with, but also because mainstream contemporary linguistics has been concerned with the formal analysis of language as an abstract system, not language as it is used in everyday life. The situation is further complicated for researchers whose individual training or fields of specialization span multiple academic disciplines.

Interdisciplinary dialogue, like all cross-cultural communication, requires compassion, flexibility, and patience, as well as the effort to understand the context from which interlocutors emerge. In light of this, I approached the task of collecting my academic writings on gender and discourse with a sense of caution. The essays gathered in this volume were originally written with my academic colleagues in mind, that is, readers in my own (already interdisciplinary) field. But I realize that they may now be read not only by colleagues in different disciplines but also by a range of readers of *You Just Don't Understand: Women and Men in Conversation* who want to see the detailed analysis and scholarly references that led to the writing of that book, as well as the theoretical discussion that was beyond its scope. So I begin by explaining my scholarly heritage and assumptions in order to contextualize the chapters that follow. In the process, this introduction also sets forth and explores some of the issues raised by a sociolinguistic, anthropologically oriented approach to gender and language—the approach that characterizes the essays in this volume.

METHODOLOGICAL CONTEXT

Within the discipline of linguistics, the work I do is referred to as "discourse analysis." This term reflects the aspect of my approach that is most significant for linguists in that it contrasts with the dominant strains in the discipline. Whereas most contemporary linguistics takes as the object of study sounds (phonetics and phonology), words (lexicon and morphology), or sentences (syntax, that is, the arrangement of words in sentences), discourse analysis focuses on connected language "beyond the sentence," as linguists often put it. On the other hand, I sometimes identify myself as a "sociolinguist," partly because I teach in the sociolinguistics program within the linguistics department at Georgetown University, but also because my work addresses the intersection of language and social phenomena.[2] Finally, I refer to my approach as anthropologically oriented because my method involves closely examining individual cases of interaction, in many of which I was a participant, and takes into account their cultural context.

The theoretical and methodological approach found here derives from the work of Robin Lakoff and John Gumperz, who were my teachers at the University of California, Berkeley. It was Lakoff (see especially Lakoff 1975, 1979, 1990) who introduced me to the concept she calls communicative style (I later began using my own term, "conversational style") and the notion that misunderstandings can arise in conversation, both cross-cultural and cross-gender, because of systematic differences in communicative style. Gumperz (see especially Gumperz 1982a) calls his type of analysis "interactional sociolinguistics" to distinguish it from the more common type of sociolinguistics that typically examines phonological variation (see Labov 1972). From Gumperz I learned the methodological approach, which is characterized by: (1) tape-recording naturally occurring conversations; (2) identifying segments in which trouble is evident; (3) looking for culturally patterned differences in signaling meaning that could account for the trouble; (4) playing the recording, or segments of it, back to participants in order to solicit their spontaneous interpretations and reactions, and also, perhaps later, soliciting their responses to the researcher's interpretations; and (5) playing segments of the interaction for other members of the cultural groups represented by the speakers in order to discern patterns of interpretation.

The last two steps are not an afterthought; they provide critical checks on interpretations, given the hermeneutic (that is, interpretive) methodological framework. They are also crucial to ensure that the scholar's work is grounded in the experience of the speakers whose behavior is the object of study. I am reminded here of Oliver Sacks, the brilliant neurologist and essayist, who demonstrates that in order to understand a medical condition, physicians need to not only examine their patients but also listen to them. Whereas modern medicine may provide invaluable insight into chemical and biological courses of disease, only patients hold the clues to what their diseases are "really like" (Sacks 1987:40). In the same spirit, attention to how participants experience conversations under analysis provides invaluable insight into the workings of interaction that are otherwise unavailable to the researcher. Furthermore, and crucially, it also provides an ethical and humanistic foundation for the research, making us accountable to those we study.

The chapters gathered here constitute the totality of my academic writings on gender and language prior to and since the publication of *You Just Don't Understand,* my eleventh book. My previous books and articles were on other topics—mostly analyzing conversation (Tannen 1984a), comparing speaking and writing (Tannen 1982a, 1982b, 1984b), and exploring the relationship between conversational and literary discourse (Tannen 1989).[3] My work on gender-related differences in conversational style is a natural development of my earlier research and writing on subcultural differences in conversational style. Thus, my approach to gender and language follows in the tradition of Gumperz and of Maltz and Borker (1982), who were similarly influenced by Gumperz. According to this view, some frustrations in conversations between women and men can be understood by reference to systematic differences in how women and men tend to signal meaning in conversation. This is quite different from the impetus behind some other work on gender and language, especially the work that grows out of a political agenda.

The roots of my approach can clearly be seen in my book *Conversational Style: Analyzing Talk Among Friends* (1984a), and dozens of articles I have published in scholarly journals and books make exactly the same claims about conversational style differences resulting in systematic misjudgments that I make in *You Just Don't Understand.* Indeed, the theoretical and methodological framework I use is found not only in the work of John Gumperz, but also in the work of others who studied with him (see the papers collected in Gumperz 1982b) or work in similar traditions. Among those who come immediately to mind are Thomas Kochman (1981) on black–white styles; Frederick Erickson (for example, Erickson and Shultz 1982, Erickson 1986), who examines the styles not only of blacks and whites but also of Italian-Americans, German-Americans, and Polish-Americans in interaction with each other; Ron and Suzanne Scollon (1981, Scollon 1985) on Athabaskan–Anglo style; and Susan Philips (1983), who compares Warm Springs Indian and Anglo styles. The list could go on and on.

THE ROLE OF DOMINANCE IN A CULTURAL DIFFERENCE FRAMEWORK

Some who are not familiar with this research tradition have misinterpreted the theoretical framework to imply that explaining the interactional consequences of style differences denies the existence of other societal forces at work. Specifically, there are those who believe that approaching gender differences in ways of speaking as "cultural" differences implies that men do not dominate women, but only misunderstand them. There is no basis for this assumption, as a glance at all the research in this tradition—including my own—makes clear. When Gumperz claims that job interviews between speakers of British English and speakers of Indian English end badly for the Pakistanis and Indians because of differences in discourse strategies, he is not denying that there are numerous and pervasive forms of discrimination against Asians in British society. When Erickson and Shultz show that white counselors end up talking down to black community college students because of differences in conventional ways of showing listenership, they are not denying that racism exists in American society, any more than Kochman denies the existence of racism when he shows systematic differences in attitudes toward "rights of expressiveness" and "rights of sensibilities" among American blacks and whites. When Susan Philips shows that Warm Springs Indian children are systematically misjudged in Anglo-taught classrooms—due, in part, to different assumptions about self-display and self-control—she is not denying that American Indians suffer many forms of discrimination in Anglo society.

Quite the opposite, every one of these scholars, like me, explicitly states that the consequences of style differences work to the disadvantage of members of groups that are stigmatized in our society, and to the advantage of those who have the power to enforce their interpretations. This is the very kernel of the term and concept of "gatekeeping"—first developed by Erickson (1975) and adopted by Gumperz—which underlies much of their own work as well as that of others working in this tradition: when style differences are found in encounters between those who hold the keys to societal power—such as community college counselors, state government representatives, or job interviewers—and those who wish to benefit from the encounter by getting career advice, governmental services, or a job, it is the person seeking benefits who systematically loses as a result of style differences. In other words, societally determined power differences are an inextricable element of cultural difference theory and research.

Another major impetus of Gumperz's work, as well as my own and that of the other scholars working in this and related traditions, is to confront and counteract the social inequality that results from negative stereotyping of minority cultural groups. Thus, when I show (Tannen 1981) that the stereotype of Jews as aggressive and pushy results in part from differences in conversational style, I am not denying that anti-Semitism exists in American society, but attempting to combat it.

Part of the cause, or perhaps the result, of this misinterpretation of the theoretical framework that approaches interactional distress as "cultural" patterning lies in an unfortunate dichotomy that has emerged in the literature, suggesting that approaches to gender and language fall into two categories: the "cultural difference" approach, as opposed to a "power" or "dominance" approach. I first became aware of this framework when I read a paper that had been presented by Nancy Henley and Cheris Kramarae at a meeting of the National Women's Studies Association in 1988. (See Henley and Kramarae [1991] for a published version.) At the time it struck me as an interesting distinction, insofar as the work of Henley, Kramarae, and others who work on gender and language in the fields of communication and sociology use dominance as the starting point of their analysis, whereas Maltz and Borker (1982) and I (the proponents of the "cultural" approach who are identified by Henley and Kramarae) use the Gumperzian framework of cultural difference as a starting point.[4] However, since I have seen this dichotomy not only referred to repeatedly by language and gender researchers but also elaborated and embroidered upon, I have come to feel that it is really a false one that obfuscates more than it clarifies. It implies that those who work in the so-called "power" or "dominance" framework have a corner on the market of hierarchical relations: if the two phenomena are conceptualized as mutually exclusive poles, then those who suggest that women's and men's styles can be understood in the framework of cultural difference are represented as denying that dominance exists. In other words, it implies that "difference" precludes "dominance," which is totally without basis.

Quite the contrary, the cultural difference framework provides a model for explaining how dominance can be created in face-to-face interaction.

It would be absurd to claim that approaching gender differences in verbal behavior as "cultural" in origin and character translates into a denial of dominance—male or any other kind. As I wrote in *You Just Don't Understand:*

> No one could deny that men as a class dominate women in our
> society, and that many individual men seek to dominate women
> in their lives. And yet male dominance is not the whole story. It
> is not sufficient to account for everything that happens to
> women and men in conversations—especially conversations in
> which both are genuinely trying to relate to each other with at-
> tention and respect. The effect of dominance is not always the
> result of an intention to dominate. (18)

In other words, far from denying the existence of dominance, exam-ining the workings of conversational style in interaction can help explain how dominance is actually created in interaction.

Indeed, the claim that such social relations as dominance and subordination are *constructed* in interaction is one of the fundamental tenets and most important contributions of the interactional socio-linguistic approach to analyzing conversation. In a way, it is the very heart of the theory underlying that approach and is exactly why interaction is seen as so important to analyze. Fundamental principles of interactional sociolinguistics include the convictions that (1) roles are not given but are created in interaction; (2) context is not given but is constituted by talk and action; (3) nothing that occurs in interaction is the sole doing of one party but rather is a "joint production," the result of the interaction of individuals' ways of speaking;[5] and, as I demonstrate in everything I've ever written and discuss directly in chapter 1, (4) linguistic features (such as interruption, volume of talk, indirectness, and so on) can never be aligned on a one-to-one basis with interactional intentions or mean-ings, in the sense that a word can be assigned a meaning. No language has meaning except by reference to how it is "framed" (Bateson 1972, Goffman 1974) or "contextualized" (Becker 1979, 1984; Gumperz 1982a).[6]

In this spirit, one of the main themes of *You Just Don't Understand* is that the systematic differences in women's and men's characteristic styles often put women in a subordinate position in interactions with men. I will give just three of innumerable specific examples. In the chapter "Lecturing and Listening" illustrating that women frequently take the role of listener and men the role of lecturer, I make the following comment:

> Once again, the alignment in which women and men find themselves arrayed is asymmetrical. The lecturer is framed as superior in status and expertise, cast in the role of teacher, and the listener is cast in the role of student. If women and men took turns giving and receiving lectures, there would be nothing disturbing about it. What is disturbing is the imbalance. . . . If men often seem to hold forth because they have the expertise, women are often frustrated and surprised to find that when they have the expertise, they don't necessarily get the floor. (125)

In a chapter on conflict I show that women's inclination to avoid conflict puts them at a disadvantage: "Women who are incapable of angry outbursts are incapable of wielding power in this way. Far worse, their avoidance of conflict opens them up to exploitation" (182–83). Finally, in a chapter on interruption I show that men often end up interrupting women because:

> men who approach conversation as a contest are likely to expend effort not to support the other's talk but to lead the conversation in another direction, perhaps one in which they can take center stage by telling a story or joke or displaying knowledge. But in doing so, they expect their conversational partners to mount resistance. Women who yield to these efforts do so not because they are weak or insecure or deferential but because they have little experience in deflecting attempts to grab the conversational wheel. (215)

The way in which my approach differs from that of the so-called "dominance theorists" is that I believe I have shown that these processes can result in dominance in conversational interaction without every individual intending to dominate in every instance. Once again, that does not deny the fact that there are numerous instances in which individuals do set out to dominate, and numerous other (nonlinguistic) sources of gender-related power differences.

BEYOND THE NATURE/NURTURE DICHOTOMY

Thus, the "cultural difference versus dominance" dichotomy misrepresents the claims and aims of the so-called "difference" framework. A similar misrepresentation lies at the heart of another source of criticism, namely, the complaint that describing gender differences in verbal behavior at all is "essentialist." This line of attack assumes that describing differences between women and men is synonymous with ascribing those differences to women's "essential" nature. This assumption, too, has no basis in the research itself and results from lack of familiarity with the intellectual framework in which linguists work.

In my own work, as in that of my colleagues in linguistics, the question of the origins of gender or other linguistic differences is not addressed. Contemporary linguistics is descriptive—our charge is to describe the patterns of language we observe—and decidedly not prescriptive. (Unlike grammarians, we don't tell anyone how they *should* speak; rather, we try to account for the ways they *do* speak. We are more like anthropologists, who approach a distant culture to understand it, than like missionaries, who seek to change it.) Thus, to describe differences is not to ascribe them to either biological or cultural sources. There are those who believe that the existence of gender differences at very early ages is evidence that these differences are biological or genetic in origin. But there are also those who argue that children of any age, even infants, are treated differently depending on their gender, and that the socialization of the group is primary, even for very young children.

Although the question of the origins of the patterns I describe has not been a focus of my concern, probably because of my anthropological orientation I have been inclined to regard socialization (that is, cultural experience) as the main influence shaping patterns of behavior. Thus, in *You Just Don't Understand,* as in the present volume, I cite research on the role of childhood peer groups as the source of gendered patterns in ways of speaking.[7]

The nature/nurture question can perhaps best be addressed by anthropological researchers who undertake large-scale cross-cultural studies. The question will certainly be addressed as well by ongoing studies of gender and the brain. Even primate studies will be brought to bear on this question. Whatever the research shows, however, people have passionate attachment to one view or the other and will necessarily differ in their interpretations of the research. Most interesting to me are the assumptions that underlie the fervent contention that differences must be primarily or even purely biological or cultural in origin. Many of those who believe—in my view, wish—the differences to be purely biological in origin assume that if this is the case, then women must be subordinate and there is no point in trying to effect social change. Many of those who believe (or wish) the differences to be purely cultural in origin assume that if this is so, they can easily change whatever they don't like in the social order. Neither of these assumptions seems justified to me. Nothing is more human than to go against nature,[8] and cultural patterns are extremely resistant to change.

What *is* required to effect change is an understanding of the patterns of human behavior as they exist today, an appreciation of the complexity of these patterns, and a humane respect for other human beings—other researchers as well as the subjects of our research. This is what I have struggled to achieve in all my work, and I hope it is evident in what follows.

The foregoing discussion is intended to clarify the theoretical background and assumptions of the approach to gender and language that characterizes the essays collected in this volume. Overviews of the individual essays, as well as discussions of the contexts in which they were originally written, are presented in headnotes preceding each chapter.

NOTES

Sincerest thanks to A. L. Becker, Ron Scollon, Michael Macovski, and Paul Friedrich for invaluable comments on a draft of this introduction.

1. I first encountered this point in an article by Henry Widdowson (1988).

2. I never thought of myself as a sociolinguist until I arrived at Georgetown. All the courses I took in my graduate program at the University of California, Berkeley, were simply linguistics classes. Moreover, I agree with Dell Hymes and others who have observed that the study of language in its social context is, after all, linguistics and should not be thought of as a "subfield."

3. The first book I wrote, *Lilika Nakos,* was a work of literary criticism, where I analyzed the fiction of a modern Greek writer in the context of her life.

4. I must admit that I was also flattered to be identified as representing a major strand of research!

5. Some key sources reflecting this view are Goodwin (1981), Schegloff (1982), McDermott and Tylbor (1983), and papers collected in Duranti and Brenneis (1986).

6. In a sense, the explication of how framing works in conversation to construct interactional meaning is the aim of all my work, but see especially the chapter "Framing" in *That's Not What I Meant! How Conversational Style Makes or Breaks Your Relations with Others* (Tannen 1986), sections on framing in *You Just Don't Understand: Women and Men in Conversation* (Tannen 1990), and my recent book *Framing in Discourse* (Tannen 1993).

7. I realize, however, that biological factors may be at work as well, and I would hope that even those who choose to examine them (of which, again, I am not one) would not be branded by the ostracizing label "essentialist," a term that is often used as a sophisticated form of academic name-calling. At best, the quest to separate privileged cultural factors from stigmatized biological factors is hopeless. As Stephen Jay Gould has reportedly put it in an interview (Angier 1993), "[B]iology and environment are inextricably linked." Gould is quoted as saying, "It's logically, mathematically, philosophically impossible to pull them apart." At worst it prevents us from examining the interrelation of these factors and impedes our understanding of human behavior. Moreover, the stigmatizing of any reference to gender differences discourages the description and understanding of human behavior as it currently exists, whereas such understanding is a necessary first step in making whatever changes we wish to effect.

8. I first heard this point made by Walter Ong at a panel discussion on spoken and written language that took place in conjunction with the Georgetown University Round Table on Languages and Linguistics 1982. I think it is not coincidental that, in my experience, those who tell me they are certain all differences are biological in origin are usually men, and those who are equally certain that they are entirely culturally based are usually women.

REFERENCES

Angier, Natalie. 1993. A scientist evolves into a celebrity. The New York Times February 11, 1993, B1, B6.

Bateson, Gregory. 1972. A theory of play and fantasy. Steps to an ecology of mind, 177–93. San Francisco: Chandler. Paperback: New York: Ballantine.

Becker, A. L. 1979. Text-building, epistemology, and aesthetics in Javanese Shadow Theatre. The imagination of reality, ed. by A. L. Becker and Aram Yengoyan, 211–43. Norwood, NJ: Ablex.

Becker, A. L. 1984. Biography of a sentence: A Burmese Proverb. Text, play, and story: The construction and reconstruction of self and society, ed. by Edward M. Bruner, 135–55. Washington, DC: American Ethnological Society. Reprinted: Prospect Heights, IL: Waveland Press.

Duranti, Alessandro, and Donald Brenneis (eds.) 1986. The audience as co-author, special issue of Text 6:3.239–47.

Erickson, Frederick. 1975. Gatekeeping and the melting pot: Interaction in counseling encounters. Harvard Educational Review 45:1.44–70.

Erickson, Frederick. 1986. Listening and speaking. Languages and linguistics: The interdependence of theory, data, and application. Georgetown University Round Table on Languages and Linguistics 1985, ed. by Deborah Tannen, 294–319. Washington, DC: Georgetown University Press.

Erickson, Frederick, and Jeffrey Shultz. 1982. The counselor as gatekeeper: Social interaction in interviews. New York: Academic Press.

Goffman, Erving. 1974. Frame analysis. New York: Harper and Row.

Goodwin, Charles. 1981. Conversational organization: Interaction between speakers and hearers. New York: Academic Press.

Gumperz, John J. 1982a. Discourse strategies. Cambridge: Cambridge University Press.

Gumperz, John J. (ed.) 1982b. Language and social identity. Cambridge: Cambridge University Press.

Henley, Nancy, and Cheris Kramarae. 1991. Miscommunicaton, gender and power. "Miscommunication" and problematic talk, ed. by Nikolas Coupland, Howard Giles, and John Wiemann. Newbury Park, CA: Sage.

Kochman, Thomas. 1981. Black and white styles in conflict. Chicago: University of Chicago Press.

Labov, William. 1972. Sociolinguistic patterns. Philadelphia: University of Pennsylvania Press.

Lakoff, Robin. 1975. Language and woman's place. New York: Harper and Row.

Lakoff, Robin Tolmach. 1979. Stylistic strategies within a grammar of style. Language, sex, and gender, ed. by Judith Orasanu, Mariam Slater, and Leonore Loeb Adler. Annals of the New York Academy of Science 327.53–78.

Lakoff, Robin Tolmach. 1990. Talking power: The politics of language in our lives. New York: Basic Books.

Maltz, Daniel N., and Ruth A. Borker. 1982. A cultural approach to male–female miscommunication. Language and social identity, ed. by John J. Gumperz, 196–216. Cambridge: Cambridge University Press.

McDermott, R. P., and Henry Tylbor. 1983. On the necessity of collusion in conversation. Text 3:3.277–97.

Philips, Susan Urmston. 1983. The invisible culture: Communication in classroom and community on the Warm Springs Indian reservation. New York: Longman.

Sacks, Oliver. 1987. Tics. The New York Review of Books, January 29, 1987, 37–41.

Schegloff, Emanuel. 1982. Discourse as an interactional achievement: Some uses of 'uhuh' and other things that come between sentences. Analyzing discourse: Text and talk. Georgetown University Round Table on Languages and Linguistics 1981, ed. by Deborah Tannen, 71–93. Washington, DC: Georgetown University Press.

Scollon, Ron. 1985. The machine stops: Silence in the metaphor of malfunction. Perspectives on silence, ed. by Deborah Tannen and Muriel Saville-Troike, 21–30. Norwood, NJ: Ablex.

Scollon, Ron, and Suzanne B. K. Scollon. 1981. Narrative, literacy and face in interethnic communication. Norwood, NJ: Ablex.

Tannen, Deborah. 1981. New York Jewish conversational style. International Journal of the Sociology of Language 30.133–39.

Tannen, Deborah. 1982a. Oral and literate strategies in spoken and written narratives. Language 58:1.1–21.

Tannen, Deborah (ed.). 1982b. Spoken and written language: Exploring orality and literacy. Norwood, NJ: Ablex.

Tannen, Deborah. 1984a. Conversational style: Analyzing talk among friends. Norwood, NJ: Ablex.

Tannen, Deborah (ed.). 1984b. Coherence in spoken and written discourse. Norwood, NJ: Ablex.

Tannen, Deborah. 1986. That's not what I meant!: How conversational style makes or breaks your relations with others. New York: William Morrow. Paperback: Ballantine.

Tannen, Deborah. 1989. Talking voices: Repetition, dialogue, and imagery in conversational discourse. Cambridge: Cambridge University Press.

Tannen, Deborah. 1990. You just don't understand: Women and men in conversation. New York: William Morrow. Paperback: Ballantine.

Tannen, Deborah. 1993. Framing in discourse. New York: Oxford University Press.

Widdowson, Henry. 1988. Poetry and pedagogy. Linguistics in context: Connecting observation and understanding, ed. by Deborah Tannen, 185–97. Norwood, NJ: Ablex.

CHAPTER ONE

The Relativity of Linguistic Strategies:
Rethinking Power and Solidarity in Gender and Dominance

In this chapter I demonstrate that the theoretical framework of power and solidarity is essential for understanding gender patterns in language use, and that gender and language is a fruitful site for investigating the dynamics underlying language choice, including such dimensions as power and solidarity. This framework is used to show that gender and language research cannot be approached as the mechanical search for specific linguistic phenomena. Using examples from conversation as well as literary creations of conversations, I argue that each of the linguistic strategies that have been claimed to show dominance can also show solidarity. For example, one can talk while another is talking in order to wrest the floor; this can be seen as a move motivated by power. Yet one can also talk along with another in order to show support and agreement; this must be seen as a move motivated by solidarity. The two, however, are not mutually exclusive. If both speakers are engaged in a ritual struggle for the floor, they might experience the entire conversation as a pleasurable one: an exercise of solidarity on the metalevel. My purpose, then, is not to question that particular linguistic strategies, such as interruption, may be used to create dominance, but rather to argue that intention and effect are not always synonymous, and that there is never an enduring one-to-one relationship betweeen a linguistic device and an interactive effect. In seeking to understand individuals' experiences of conversation, including dominance, we will have to look more deeply and more subtly at the workings of conversational interaction.

INTRODUCTION

IN ANALYZING DISCOURSE, many researchers operate on the unstated assumption that all speakers proceed along similar lines of interpretation, so a particular example of discourse can be taken to represent how discourse works for all speakers. For some aspects of discourse, this is undoubtedly true. Yet a large body of sociolinguistic literature makes clear that, for many aspects of discourse, this is so only to the extent that cultural background is shared. To the extent that cultural backgrounds differ, lines of interpretation and habitual use of many linguistic strategies are likely to diverge. One thinks immediately and minimally of the work of Gumperz (1982), Erickson and Shultz (1982), Scollon and Scollon (1981), and Philips (1983). My own research shows that cultural difference is not limited to the gross and apparent levels of country of origin and native language, but also exists at the subcultural levels of ethnic heritage, class, geographic region, age, and gender. My earlier work (Tannen 1984, 1986) focuses on ethnic and regional style; my most recent work (Tannen 1990) focuses on gender-related stylistic variation. I draw on this work here to demonstrate that specific linguistic strategies have widely divergent potential meanings.[1]

This insight is particularly significant for research on language and gender, much of which has sought to describe the linguistic means by which men dominate women in interaction. That men dominate women is not in question; what I am problematizing is the source and workings of domination and other interpersonal intentions and effects. I will show that one cannot locate the source of domination, or of any interpersonal intention or effect, in linguistic strategies such as interruption, volubility, silence, and topic raising, as has been claimed. Similarly, one cannot locate the source of women's powerlessness in such linguistic strategies as indirectness, taciturnity, silence, and tag questions, as has also been claimed. The reason one cannot do this is that the same linguistic means can be used for different, even opposite, purposes and can have different, even opposite, effects in different contexts. Thus, a strategy that seems, or is, intended to dominate may in another context or in the mouth of another speaker be intended or used to establish connection. Similarly, a strategy that seems, or is, intended to create connection can in another context or in the mouth of another speaker be intended or used to establish dominance.

Put another way, the "true" intention or motive of any utterance cannot be determined from examination of linguistic form alone. For one thing, intentions and effects are not identical. For another, as the sociolinguistic literature has dramatized repeatedly (see especially McDermott and Tylbor 1983; Schegloff 1982, 1988; Erickson 1986; Duranti and Brenneis 1986), human interaction is a "joint production": everything that occurs results from the interaction of all participants. The source of the ambiguity and polysemy of linguistic strategies that I will explore here is the paradoxical relationship between the dynamics of power and solidarity.

OVERVIEW OF THE CHAPTER

In this chapter I first briefly explain the theoretical paradigm of power and solidarity. Then I show that linguistic strategies are potentially ambiguous (they could "mean" either power or solidarity) and polysemous (they could "mean" both). Third, I reexamine and expand the power and solidarity framework in light of cross-cultural research. Finally, I demonstrate the relativity of five linguistic strategies: indirectness, interruption, silence versus volubility, topic raising, and adversativeness (that is, verbal conflict).

THEORETICAL BACKGROUND

Power and Solidarity

Since Brown and Gilman's (1960) introduction of the concept and subsequent elaborations of it, especially those of Friedrich (1972) and Brown and Levinson ([1978]1987), the dynamics of power and solidarity have been fundamental to sociolinguistic theory. (Fasold [1990] provides an overview.) Brown and Gilman based their framework on analysis of the use of pronouns in European languages which have two forms of the second person pronoun, such as the French *tu* and *vous*. In English the closest parallel is to be found in forms of address: first name versus title–last name. In Brown and Gilman's system, power is associated with nonreciprocal use of pronouns; in English the parallel would be a situation in which one speaker addresses the other by first name but is addressed by title–last name (for example, doctor and patient, teacher and student, boss and secretary, building resident and elevator operator). Solidarity is associated with reciprocal pronoun use or symmetrical forms of address: both speakers address each other by *tu* or by *vous* (in English, by title–last name or by first name). Power governs asymmetrical relationships where one is subordinate to another; solidarity governs symmetrical relationships characterized by social equality and similarity.

In my previous work exploring the relationship between power and solidarity as it emerges in conversational discourse (Tannen 1984, 1986), I note that power and solidarity are in paradoxical relation to each other. That is, although power and solidarity, closeness and distance, seem at first to be opposites, each also entails the other. Any show of solidarity necessarily entails power, in that the requirement of similarity and closeness limits freedom and independence. At the same time, any show of power entails solidarity by involving participants in relation to each other. This creates a close-ness that can be contrasted with the distance of individuals who have no relation to each other at all.

In Brown and Gilman's paradigm, the key to power is asymmetry, but it is often thought to be formality. This is seen in the following anecdote. I once entitled a lecture "The Paradox of Power and Solidarity." The respondent to my talk appeared wearing a three-piece suit and a knapsack on his back. The audience was amused by the association of the suit with power, the knapsack with solidarity. There was something immediately recognizable in this semiotic. Indeed, a professor wearing a knapsack might well mark solidarity with students at, for example, a protest demonstration. And wearing a three-piece suit to the demonstration might mark power by differentiating the wearer from the demonstrators, perhaps even reminding them of his dominant position in the institutional hierarchy. But wearing a three-piece suit to the board meeting of a corporation would mark solidarity with other board members, whereas wearing a knapsack in that setting would connote not solidarity but disrespect, a move in the power dynamic.

The Ambiguity of Linguistic Strategies

As the preceding example shows, the same symbol—a three-piece suit—can signal either power or solidarity, depending on, at least, the setting (for example, a board meeting or student demonstration), the habitual dress style of the individual, and the comparison of his clothing with that worn by others in the interaction. (I say "his" intentionally; the range of meanings would be quite different if a man's three-piece suit were worn by a woman.) This provides an analogue to the ambiguity of linguistic strategies, which are signals in the semiotic system of language. As I have demonstrated at length in previous books (see especially Tannen 1984, 1986, 1990), all linguistic strategies are potentially ambiguous. The power–solidarity dynamic is one fundamental source of ambiguity. What appear as attempts to dominate a conversation (an exercise of power) may actually be intended to establish rapport (an exercise of solidarity). This occurs because (as I have worded it elsewhere) power and solidarity are bought with the same currency: The same linguistic means can be used to create either or both.

This ambiguity can be seen in the following fleeting conversation. Two women were walking together from one building to another in order to attend a meeting. They were joined by a man they both knew who had just exited a third building on his way to the same meeting. One of the women greeted the man and remarked, "Where's your coat?" The man responded, "Thanks, Mom." His response framed the woman's remark as a gambit in a power exchange: a mother tells a child to put on his coat. Yet the woman might have intended the remark as showing friendly concern rather than parental caretaking. Was it power (condescending, on the model of parent to child) or solidarity (friendly, on the model of intimate peers)? Though the man's uptake is clear, the woman's intention in making the remark is not.

Another example comes from a letter written to me by a reader of *You Just Don't Understand: Women and Men in Conversation*. A woman was at home when her partner arrived and announced that his archrival had invited him to contribute a chapter to a book. The woman remarked cheerfully how nice it was that the rival was initiating a rapprochement by including her partner in his book. He told her she had got it wrong: because the rival would be the editor and he merely a contributor, the rival was actually trying to solidify his dominance. She interpreted the invitation in terms of solidarity. He interpreted it as an expression of power. Which was right? I don't know. The invitation was ambiguous; it could have "meant" either. I suspect it had elements of both. In other words, it was polysemous.

The Polysemy of Power and Solidarity

If ambiguity denotes meaning one thing *or* another, polysemy denotes meaning one thing *and* another—that is, having multiple meanings simultaneously. The question "Where's your coat?" shows friendly concern *and* suggests a parent–child constellation. The invitation to contribute a chapter to a book brings editor and contributor closer *and* suggests a hierarchical relationship.

One more example will illustrate the polysemy of strategies signaling power and solidarity. If you have a friend who repeatedly picks up the check when you dine together, is she being generous and sharing her wealth, or is she trying to flaunt her money and remind you that she has more of it than you? Although the intention may be to make you feel good by her generosity, her repeated generosity may nonetheless make you feel bad by reminding you that she has more money. Thus, both of you are caught in the web of the ambiguity of power and solidarity. It is impossible to determine which was her real motive, and whether it justifies your response. On the other hand, even if you believe her motive was purely generous, you may nonetheless feel denigrated by her generosity because the fact that she has this generous impulse is evidence that she has more money than you, and her expressing the impulse reminds you of it. In other words, both interpretations exist at once: solidarity (she is paying to be nice) and power (her being nice in this way reminds you that she is richer). In this sense, the strategy is not just ambiguous with regard to power and solidarity but polysemous. This polysemy explains another observation that initially surprised me: Paules (1991) reports that waitresses in the restaurant where she did ethnographic field work were offended not only by tips that were too small, but also by tips that were too large. The customers' inordinate beneficence implies that the amount of money left is insignificant to the tipper but significant to the waitress.

Brown and Gilman are explicit in their assumption that power is associated with asymmetrical relationships in which the power is held by the person in the one-up position. This is stated in their definition:

> One person may be said to have power over another to the degree that he is able to control the behavior of the other. Power

is a relationship between at least two persons, and it is non-reciprocal in the sense that both cannot have power in the same area of behavior. (255)

I have called attention, however, to the extent to which solidarity in itself can be a form of control. For example, a young woman complained about friends who "don't let you be different." If the friend says she has a particular problem and the woman says, "I don't have that problem," her friend is hurt and accuses her of putting her down, of acting superior. The assumption of similarity requires the friend to have a matching problem.[2]

Furthermore, although Brown and Gilman acknowledge that "power superiors may be solidary (parents, elder siblings)" and "power inferiors, similarly, may be as solidary as the old family retainer" (258), most Americans are inclined to assume that solidarity implies closeness, whereas power implies distance.[3] Thus Americans regard the sibling relationship as the ultimate in solidarity: "sister" or "brother" are often used metaphorically to indicate closeness and equality.[4] In contrast, it is often assumed that hierarchy precludes closeness: employers and employees cannot "really" be friends. But being linked in a hierarchy necessarily brings individuals closer. This is an assumption underlying Watanabe's (1993) observation, in comparing American and Japanese group discussions, that whereas the Americans in her study saw themselves as individuals participating in a joint activity, the Japanese saw themselves as members of a group united by hierarchy. When reading Watanabe, I was caught up short by the term "united." My inclination had been to assume that hierarchy is distancing, not uniting.

The anthropological literature includes numerous discussions of cultural contexts in which hierarchical relationships are seen as close and mutually, not unilaterally, empowering. For example, Beeman (1986) describes an Iranian interactional pattern he dubs "getting the lower hand." Taking the lower-status position enables an Iranian to invoke a protector schema by which the higher-status person is obligated to do things for him or her. Similarly, Yamada (1992) describes the Japanese relationship of *amae,* typified by the parent–child or employer–employee constellation. It binds two individuals in a hierarchical interdependence by which both have power in the form of obligations as well as rights vis-à-vis the other. Finally, Wolfowitz (1991) explains that respect/deference is experienced by Suriname Javanese not as subservience but as an assertion of claims.

The Suriname Javanese example is particularly intriguing because it calls into question the association of asymmetry with power and distance. The style Wolfowitz calls respect politeness is characterized by both social closeness and negative politeness.[5] It is hierarchical insofar as it is directional and unequal; however, the criterion for directionality is not status but age. The prototypical relationship characterized by respect politeness is grandchild–grandparent: a relationship that is both highly unequal and very close. Moreover, according to Wolfowitz, the Javanese assume that familial relations are inherently hierarchical, including age-graded siblings. Equality, in contrast, is associated with formal relationships that are also marked by social distance.

We can display these dynamics in the following way. The model that reflects American assumptions conceptualizes power and solidarity as opposite ends of a single continuum simultaneously representing symmetry/asymmetry, hierarchy/equality, and distance/closeness. (See figure 1.1.) In contrast, the cross-cultural perspective suggests a multidimensional grid of at least (and, potentially and probably, more) intersecting continua. The closeness/

power	solidarity
asymmetry	symmetry
hierarchy	equality
distance	closeness

Figure 1.1. *Unidimensional model*

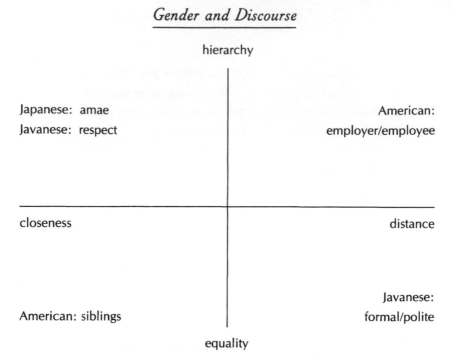

Figure 1.2. *Multidimensional model*

distance dimension can be placed on one axis and the hierarchy/ equality one on another. (See figure 1.2.) Indeed, the intersection of these dimensions—that is, the co-incidence of hierarchy and closeness—may account, at least in part, for what I am calling the ambiguity and polysemy of power and solidarity.

Similarity/Difference

There is one more aspect of the dynamics of power and solidarity that bears discussion before I demonstrate the relativity of linguistic strategies. That is the similarity/difference continuum and its relation to the other dynamics discussed.

For Brown and Gilman, solidarity implies sameness, in contrast to power, about which they observe, "In general terms, the *V* form is linked with differences between persons" (256). This is explicit in their definition of "the solidarity semantic":

Now we are concerned with a new set of relations which are symmetrical; for example, *attended the same school* or *have the same parents* or *practice the same profession.* If A has the same parents as B, B has the same parents as A. Solidarity is the name we give to the general relationship and solidarity is symmetrical. (257; italics in original)

The similarity/difference continuum calls to mind what I have discussed elsewhere (Tannen 1984, 1986) as the double bind of communication.[6] In some ways, we are all the same. But in other ways we are all different. Communication is a double bind in the sense that anything we say to honor our similarity violates our difference, and anything we say to honor our difference violates our sameness. Thus a complaint can be lodged: "Don't think I'm different." ("If you prick me, do I not bleed?" one might protest, like Shylock.) But a complaint can also be lodged: "Don't think I'm the same." (Thus, women who have primary responsibility for the care of small children may be effectively excluded from activities and events at which day care is not provided.) Becker (1982:125) expresses this double bind as "a matter of continual self-correction between exuberance (that is, friendliness: you are like me) and deficiency (that is, respect: you are not me)." All these formulations elaborate on the tension between similarity and difference, or what Becker and Oka (1974) call "the cline of person," a semantic dimension they suggest may be the one most basic to language; that is, one deals with the world and the objects and people in it in terms of how close (and, I would add, similar) they are to oneself.

As a result of these dynamics, similarity is a threat to hierarchy. This is dramatized in Harold Pinter's play *Mountain Language.* Composed of four brief scenes, the play is set in a political prison in the capital city of an unnamed country that is under dictatorial siege. In the second scene, an old mountain woman is finally allowed to visit her son across a table as a guard stands over them. But whenever she tries to speak to her son, the guard silences her, telling the prisoner to tell his mother that it is forbidden to speak their mountain language in the capital. Then he continues: (Spaced dots indicate omitted text; unspaced dots are a form of punctuation included in the original text.)

> GUARD
>
> . . . And I'll tell you another thing. I've got a wife and three kids. And you're all a pile of shit.
>
> *Silence.*
>
> PRISONER
>
> I've got a wife and three kids.
>
> GUARD
>
> You've what?
>
> *Silence.*
>
> You've got what?
>
> *Silence.*
>
> What did you say to me? You've got what?
>
> *Silence.*
>
> You've got *what?*
>
> *He picks up the telephone and dials one digit.*
>
> Sergeant? I'm in the Blue Room ... yes ... I thought I should report, Sergeant ... I think I've got a joker in here.

The Sergeant soon enters and asks, "What joker?" The stage darkens and the scene ends. The final scene opens on the same setting, with the prisoner bloody and shaking, his mother shocked into speechlessness.

The prisoner was beaten for saying, "I've got a wife and three kids." This quotidian statement, which would be unremarkable in casual conversation, was insubordinate in the hierarchical context of brutal oppression because the guard had just made the same statement. When the guard said, "I've got a wife and three kids. And you're a pile of shit," he was claiming, "I am different from you." One could further interpret his words to imply, "I'm human, and you're not. Therefore I have a right to dominate and abuse you." By repeating the guard's words verbatim, the prisoner was then saying, "I am the same as you."[7] By claiming *his* humanity and implicitly denying the guard's assertion that he is "a pile of shit," the prisoner challenged the guard's right to dominate him.[8] Similarity is antithetical to hierarchy.

The ambiguity of closeness, a spatial metaphor representing similarity or involvement, emerges in a nonverbal aspect of this scene. In the performance I saw, the guard moved steadily closer to the prisoner as he repeated the question "You've got what?" until he was bending over him, nose to nose. The guard's moving closer was a kinesic/proxemic analogue to the prisoner's statement, but with opposite effect: he was "closing in." The guard moved closer and brought his face into contact with the prisoner's not as a sign of affection (which such actions could signify in another context) but as a threat. Closeness, then, can mean aggression rather than affiliation in the context of a hierarchical rather than symmetrical relationship.

THE RELATIVITY OF LINGUISTIC STRATEGIES

The potential ambiguity of linguistic strategies to mark both power and solidarity in face-to-face interaction has made mischief in language and gender research, wherein it is tempting to assume that whatever women do results from, or creates, their powerlessness and whatever men do results from, or creates, their dominance. But all the linguistic strategies that have been taken by analysts as evidence of subordination can in some circumstances be instruments of affiliation. For the remainder of this chapter I demonstrate the relativity of linguistic strategies by considering each of the following strategies in turn: indirectness, interruption, silence versus volubility, topic raising, and adversativeness or verbal conflict. All of these strategies have been "found" by researchers to express or create dominance or subordination. I will demonstrate that they are ambiguous or polysemous with regard to dominance/subordination (that is, power) or distance/closeness (that is, solidarity). Once again, I am not arguing that these strategies *cannot* be used to create dominance or powerlessness, much less that dominance and powerlessness do not exist. Rather, my purpose is to demonstrate that the "meaning" of any linguistic strategy can vary, depending at least on context, the conversational styles of participants, and the interaction of participants' styles and strategies. Therefore the operation of specific linguistic strategies must be studied more closely to understand how dominance and powerlessness are expressed and created in interaction.

Indirectness

Lakoff (1975) identifies two benefits of indirectness: defensiveness and rapport. Defensiveness refers to a speaker's preference not to go on record with an idea in order to be able to disclaim, rescind, or modify it if it does not meet with a positive response. The rapport benefit of indirectness results from the pleasant experience of getting one's way not because one demanded it (power) but because the other person wanted the same thing (solidarity). Many researchers have focused on the defensive or power benefit of indirectness and ignored the payoff in rapport or solidarity.

The claim by Conley, O'Barr, and Lind (1979) that women's language is really powerless language has been particularly influential. In this view, women's tendency to be indirect is taken as evidence that women don't feel entitled to make demands. Surely there are cases in which this is true. Yet it can also be demonstrated that those who feel entitled to make demands may prefer not to, seeking the payoff in rapport. Furthermore, the ability to get one's demands met without expressing them directly can be a sign of power rather than of the lack of it. An example I have used elsewhere (Tannen 1986, this volume, chapter 5) is the Greek father who answers, "If you want, you can go," to his daughter's inquiry about going to a party. Because of the lack of enthusiasm of his response, the Greek daughter understands that her father would prefer she not go and "chooses" not to go. (A "real" approval would have been "Yes, of course, you should go.") I argue that this father did not feel power-less to give his daughter orders. Rather, a communicative system was conventionalized by which he and she could both preserve the appearance, and possibly the belief, that she chose not to go rather than simply obeying his command.

Far from being powerless, this father felt so powerful that he did not need to give his daughter orders; he simply needed to let her know his preference, and she would accommodate to it. By this reasoning, indirectness is a prerogative of the powerful. By the same reasoning a master who says, "It's cold in here," may expect a servant to make a move to close a window, but a servant who says the same thing is not likely to see his employer rise to correct the situation and make him more comfortable. Indeed, a Frenchman who was raised in Brittany tells me that his family never gave bald commands to their servants but always communicated orders in indirect and highly polite form. This pattern renders less surprising the finding of Bellinger and Gleason (1982, reported in Gleason 1987) that fathers' speech to their young children had a higher incidence than mothers' of both direct imperatives (such as "Turn the bolt with the wrench") *and* implied indirect imperatives (for example, "The wheel is going to fall off").

The use of indirectness can hardly be understood without the cross-cultural perspective. Many Americans find it self-evident that directness is logical and aligned with power whereas indirectness is akin to dishonesty as well as subservience. But for speakers raised in most of the world's cultures, varieties of indirectness are the norm in communication. In Japanese interaction, for example, it is well known that saying "no" is considered too face-threatening to risk, so negative responses are phrased as positive ones: one never says "no," but listeners understand from the form of the "yes" whether it is truly a "yes" or a polite "no."

The American tendency to associate indirectness with female style is not culturally universal. The above description of typical Japanese style operates for men as well as women. My own research (Tannen 1981, 1984, 1986) suggests that Americans of some cultural and geographic backgrounds, female as well as male, are more likely than others to use relatively direct rather than indirect styles. In an early study (see chapter 5) I compared Greeks and Americans with regard to their tendency to interpret a question as an indirect means of making a request. I found that whereas American women were more likely to take an indirect interpretation of a sample conversation, Greek men were as likely as Greek women, and more likely than American men *or women,* to take an indirect interpretation. Greek men, of course, are not less powerful vis-à-vis women than American men.

Perhaps most striking is the finding of Keenan (1974) that in a Malagasy-speaking village on the island of Madagascar, women are seen as direct and men as indirect. But this in no way implies that the women are more powerful than men in this society. Quite the contrary, Malagasy men are socially dominant, and their indirect style is more highly valued. Keenan found that women were widely believed to debase the language with their artless directness, whereas men's elaborate indirectness was widely admired.

Indirectness, then, is not in itself a strategy of subordination. Rather, it can be used either by the powerful or the powerless. The interpretation of a given utterance, and the likely response to it, depends on the setting, on individuals' status and their relationship to each other, and also on the linguistic conventions that are ritualized in the cultural context.

Interruption

That interruption is a sign of dominance has been as widespread an assumption in research as in conventional wisdom. One rarely encounters an article on gender and language that does not make this claim. Most frequently cited is West and Zimmerman's (1983) finding that men dominate women by interrupting them in conversation. Tellingly, however, Deborah James and Sandra Clarke (1993), reviewing research on gender and interruption, do not find a clear pattern of males interrupting females. Especially significant is their observation that studies comparing amount of interruption in all-female versus all-male conversations find more interruption, not less, in all-female groups. Though initially surprising, this finding reinforces the need to distinguish linguistic strategies by their interactional purpose. Does the overlap show support for the speaker, or does it contradict or change the topic? I explore this phenomenon in detail in chapter 2 of this volume, but I will include a brief summary of the argument here.

The phenomenon commonly referred to as "interruption," but which is more accurately referred to as "overlap," is a paradigm case of the ambiguity of power and solidarity. This is clearly demonstrated with reference to a two-and-a-half-hour Thanksgiving dinner conversation that I analyzed at length (Tannen 1984). My analysis makes clear that some speakers consider talking along with another to be a show of enthusiastic participation in the conversation, of solidarity, creating connections; others, however, assume that only one voice should be heard at a time, so for them any overlap is an interruption, an attempt to wrest the floor, a power play. The result, in the conversation I analyzed, was that enthusiastic listeners who overlapped cooperatively, talking along to establish rapport, were perceived by overlap-resistant speakers as interrupting. This doubtless contributed to the impression reported by the overlap-resistant speakers that the cooperative overlappers had "dominated" the conversation. Indeed, the tape and transcript also give the impression that the cooperative overlappers had dominated, because the overlap-aversant participants tended to stop speaking as soon as another voice began.

It is worth emphasizing the role of symmetry, or balance, in determining whether an overlap becomes an interruption in the negative or power-laden sense. If one speaker repeatedly overlaps and another repeatedly gives way, the resulting communication is unbalanced, or asymmetrical, and the effect (though not necessarily the intent) is domination. But if both speakers avoid overlap, or if both speakers overlap each other and win out equally, there is symmetry and no domination, regardless of speakers' intentions. In an important sense, though—and this will be discussed in the last section under the rubric of adversativeness—the very engagement in a symmetrical struggle for the floor can be experienced as creating rapport, in the spirit of ritual opposition analogous to sports. Further, an imbalance can result from differences in the purpose for which overlap is used. If one speaker tends to talk along in order to show support, and the other chimes in to take the floor, the floor-taking overlapper will tend to dominate.

Thus, to understand whether an overlap is an interruption, one must consider the context (for example, cooperative overlapping is more likely to occur in casual conversation among friends than in a job interview), speakers' habitual styles (for example, overlaps are more likely not to be interruptions among those with a style I call "high involvement"), and the interaction of their styles (for example, an interruption is more likely to occur between speakers whose styles differ with regard to pausing and overlap). This is not to say that one cannot use interruption to dominate a conversation or a person, but only that it is not self-evident from the observation of overlap that an interruption has occurred, was intended, or was intended to dominate.

Silence Versus Volubility

The excerpt from Pinter's *Mountain Language* dramatizes the assumption that powerful people do the talking and powerless people are silenced. This is the trope that underlies the play's title and its central theme: By outlawing their language, the oppressors silence the mountain people, robbing them of their ability to speak and hence of their humanity. In the same spirit, many scholars (for example, Spender 1980) have claimed that men dominate women by silencing them. There are obviously circumstances in which this is accurate. Coates (1986) notes numerous proverbs that instruct women, like children, to be silent.

Silence alone, however, is not a self-evident sign of powerlessness, nor volubility a self-evident sign of domination. A theme running through Komarovsky's (1962) classic study of *Blue-Collar Marriage* is that many of the wives interviewed said they talked more than their husbands: "He's tongue-tied," one woman said (13); "My husband has a great habit of not talking," said another (162); "He doesn't say much but he means what he says and the children mind him," said a third (353). Yet there is no question but that these husbands are dominant in their marriages, as the last of these quotes indicates.

Indeed, taciturnity itself can be an instrument of power. This is precisely the claim of Sattel (1983), who argues that men use silence to exercise power over women. Sattel illustrates with a scene from Erica Jong's novel *Fear of Flying,* only a brief part of which is presented here. The first line of dialogue is spoken by Isadora, the second by her husband, Bennett. (Spaced dots indicate omitted text; unspaced dots are a form of punctuation included in the original text.)

"Why do you turn on me? What did I do?"
Silence.
"What did I do?"
He looks at her as if her not knowing were another in-jury.
"Look, let's just go to sleep now. Let's just forget it."
"Forget what?"
He says nothing.

. . .

"It was something in the movie, wasn't it?"
"What, in the movie?"
". . . It was the funeral scene. ... The little boy looking at his dead mother. Something got you there. That was when you got depressed."
Silence.
"Well, *wasn't* it?"
Silence.
"Oh come on, Bennett, you're making me *furious.* Please tell me. Please."

The painful scene continues in this vein until Bennett tries to leave the room and Isadora tries to detain him. The excerpt certainly seems to support Sattel's claim that Bennett's silence subjugates his wife, as the scene ends with her literally lowered to the floor, clinging to his pajama leg. But the reason his silence is an effective weapon is her insistence that he tell her what's wrong. If *she* receded into silence, leaving the room or refusing to talk to him, his silence would be disarmed. The devastation results not from his silence alone but from the interaction of his silence and her insistence on talking, in other words, the interaction of their differing styles.[9]

Researchers have counted numbers of words spoken or timed length of talk in order to demonstrate that men talk more than women and thereby dominate interactions. (See James and Drakich 1993 for a summary of research on amount of talk.) Undoubtedly there is truth to this observation in some settings. But the association of volubility with dominance does not hold for all settings and all cultures. Imagine, for example, an interrogation, in which the interrogator does little of the talking but holds all the power.

The relativity of the "meaning" of taciturnity and volubility is highlighted in Margaret Mead's (1977) discussion of "end linkage," a concept developed jointly by Mead, Gregory Bateson, and Geoffrey Gorer. The claim is that universal and biologically constructed relationships, such as parent–child, are linked to different behaviors in different cultures. One of their paradigm examples is the apportionment of spectatorship and exhibitionism. In middle-class American culture, children, who are obviously the weaker party in the constellation, are expected to exhibit while their more powerful parents are spectators. (Consider, for example, the American child who is prompted to demonstrate how well s/he can recite the alphabet for guests.) In contrast, in middle- and upper-class British culture, exhibition is associated with the parental role and spectatorship with children, who are expected to be seen and not heard.

Moreover, volubility and taciturnity, too, can result from style differences rather than speakers' intentions. As I (Tannen 1984, 1985) and others (Scollon and Scollon 1981, Scollon 1985) have discussed, there are cultural and subcultural differences in the length of pauses expected between and within speaking turns. In my study of the dinner conversation, those who expected shorter pauses between conversational turns began to feel an uncomfortable silence ensuing while their longer-pausing friends were simply waiting for what they regarded as the "normal" end-of-turn pause. The result was that the shorter pausers ended up doing most of the talking, another sign interpreted by their interlocutors as dominating the conversation. But their intentions had been to fill in what to them were potentially uncomfortable silences, that is, to grease the conversational wheels and ensure the success of the conversation. In their view, the taciturn participants were uncooperative, failing to do their part to maintain the conversation.

Thus, silence and volubility cannot always be taken to "mean" power or powerlessness, domination or subjugation. Rather, both may imply either power or solidarity, depending on the dynamics discussed.

Topic Raising

Shuy (1982) is typical in assuming that the speaker who raises the most topics is dominating a conversation. However, in a study I conducted (see this volume, chapter 3) of videotaped conversations among friends of varying ages recorded by Dorval (1990), it emerged that the speaker who raised the most topics was not always dominant, as judged by other criteria (for example, who took the lead in addressing the investigator when he entered the room?). In a 20-minute conversation between a pair of sixth-grade girls who identified themselves as best friends, Shannon raised the topic of Julia's relationship with Mary by saying, "Too bad you and Mary are not good friends anymore." The conversation proceeded and continued to focus almost exclusively on Julia's troubled relationship with Mary.

Similarly, most of the conversation between two tenth-grade girls was about Nancy, but Sally raised the topic of Nancy's problems. In response to Nancy's question "Well, what do you want to talk about?" Sally said, "Your mama. Did you talk to your mama?" The ensuing conversation focuses on events involving Nancy's mother and boyfriend. Overall, Sally raised nine topics, Nancy seven. However, all but one of the topics Sally raised were questions focused on Nancy. If raising more topics is a sign of dominance, Sally controlled the conversation when she raised topics, although even this was subject to Nancy's collaboration by picking them up. It may or may not be the case that Sally controlled the conversation, but the nature of her dominance is surely other than what is normally assumed by that term if the topics she raised were all about Nancy.

Finally, the effect of raising topics may also be an effect of differences in pacing and pausing, as discussed above with regard to my study of dinner-table conversation. A speaker who thinks the other has no more to say on a given topic may try to contribute to the conversation by raising another topic. But a speaker who was intending to say more and was simply waiting for the appropriate turn-exchange pause will feel that the floor was taken away and the topic aggressively switched. Yet again, the impression of dominance might result from style differences.

Adversativeness: Conflict and Verbal Aggression

Research on gender and language has consistently found male speakers to be competitive and more likely to engage in conflict (for example, by arguing, issuing commands, and taking opposing stands) and females to be cooperative and more likely to avoid conflict (for example, by agreeing, supporting, and making suggestions rather than commands). (Maltz and Borker [1982] summarize some of this research.) Ong (1981:51) argues that "adversativeness" is universal, but "conspicuous or expressed adversativeness is a larger element in the lives of males than of females."

In my analysis of videotapes of male and female friends talking to each other (this volume, chapter 3), I have begun to investigate how male adversativeness and female cooperation are played out, complicated, and contradicted in conversational discourse. In analyzing videotapes of friends talking, for example, I found a sixth-grade boy saying to his best friend,

> Seems like, if there's a fight, me and you are automatically in it. And everyone else wants to go against you and everything. It's hard to agree without someone saying something to you.

In contrast, girls of the same age (and also of most other ages whose talk I examined) spent a great deal of time discussing the dangers of anger and contention. In affirming their own friendship, one girl told her friend,

> Me and you <u>never</u> get in fights hardly,

and

> I mean like if I try to talk to you, you'll say, 'Talk to <u>me</u>!' And if you try to talk to me, I'll <u>talk</u> to you.

These examples of gendered styles of interaction are illuminated by the insight that power and solidarity are mutually evocative. As seen in the statement of the sixth-grade boy, opposing other boys in teams entails affiliation within the team. The most dramatic instance of male affiliation resulting from conflict with others is bonding among soldiers, a phenomenon explored by Norman (1990).

By the same token, girls' efforts to support their friends necessarily entail exclusion of or opposition to other girls. This emerges in Hughes' (1988) study of girls playing a street game called four-square, in which four players occupy one square each and bounce a ball into each other's squares. The object of the game is to eliminate players by hitting the ball into their square in such a way that they fail to hit it back. But this effort to "get people out" is at odds with the social injunction under which the girls operate, to be "nice" and not "mean." Hughes found that the girls resolved the conflict, and formed "incipient teams" composed of friends, by claiming that their motivation in eliminating some players was to enable others (their friends) to enter the game, since eliminated players are replaced by awaiting players. In the girls' terms, "getting someone out" was "nice-mean," because it was reframed as "getting someone [a friend] in." This dynamic is also supported by my analysis of the sixth-grade girls' conversation: Most of their talk was devoted to allying themselves with each other in opposition to another girl who was not present. So their cooperation (solidarity) also entails opposition (power).

For boys power entails solidarity not only by opposition to another team, but by opposition to each other. In the videotapes of friends talking, I found that all the conversations between young boys (and none between young girls) had numerous examples of teasing and mock attack.[10] In examining preschool conversations transcribed and analyzed by Corsaro and Rizzo (1990:34), I was amazed to discover that a fight could initiate rather than preclude friendship. In the following episode, a little boy intrudes on two others and an angry fight ensues. This is the way Corsaro and Rizzo present the dialogue:

> *Two boys (Richard and Denny) have been playing with a slinky on the stairway leading to the upstairs playhouse in the school. During their play two other boys (Joseph and Martin) enter and stand near the bottom of the stairs.*
>
> Denny: Go!
>
> *(Martin now runs off, but Joseph remains and he eventually moves halfway up the stairs.)*
>
> Joseph: These are big shoes.
>
> Richard: I'll punch him right in the eye.
>
> Joseph: I'll punch you right in the nose.
>
> Denny: I'll punch him with my big fist.
>
> Joseph: I'll-I-I-
>
> Richard: And he'll be bumpety, bumpety and punched out all the way down the stairs.

Joseph: I-I- I'll- I could poke your eyes out with my gun. I have a gun.

Denny: A gun! I'll- I- I- even if-

Richard: I have a gun too.

Denny: And I have guns too and it's bigger than yours and it poo-poo down. That's poo-poo.

(*All three boys laugh at Denny's reference to poo-poo.*)

Richard: Now leave.

Joseph: Un-uh. I gonna tell you to put on- on the gun on your hair and the poop will come right out on his face.

Denny: Well.

Richard: Slinky will snap right on your face too.

Denny: And my gun will snap right-

Up until this point I had no difficulty interpreting the interaction: The boys were engaged in a fight occasioned by Joseph's intrusion into Richard and Denny's play. But what happened next surprised and, at first, perplexed me. Corsaro and Rizzo describe it this way:

> At this point a girl (Debbie) enters, says she is Batgirl, and asks if they have seen Robin. Joseph says he is Robin, but she says she is looking for a different Robin and then runs off. After Debbie leaves, Denny and Richard move into the playhouse and Joseph follows. From this point to the end of the episode the three boys play together.

At first I was incredulous that so soon after their seemingly hostile encounter, the boys played amicably together. I finally came to the conclusion that for Joseph picking a fight was a way to enter into interaction with the other boys, and engaging him in the fight was Richard and Denny's way of accepting him into their interaction—at least after he acquitted himself satisfactorily in the fight. In this light, I could see that the reference to poo-poo, which occasioned general laughter, was the beginning of a reframing from fighting to playing.[11]

Folklore provides numerous stories in which fighting precipitates friendship among men. One such is attributed by Bly (1990:243–44) to Joseph Campbell's account of the Sumerian epic, *Gilgamesh*. In Bly's rendition, Gilgamesh, a young king, wants to befriend a wild man named Enkidu. When Enkidu is told of Gilgamesh,

> his heart grew light. He yearned for a friend. "Very well!" he said. "And I shall challenge him."

Bly paraphrases the continuation: "Enkidu then travels to the city and meets Gilgamesh; the two wrestle, Enkidu wins, and the two become inseparable friends."[12]

A modern-day academic equivalent to the bonding that results from opposition is to be found in the situation of fruitful collaborations that began when an audience member publicly challenged a speaker after his talk. Finally, Penelope Eckert (personal communication) informs me that in her research on high school students (Eckert 1990) she was told by boys, but never by girls, that their close friendships began by fighting.

These examples call into question the correlation of aggression and power on one hand, and cooperation and solidarity on the other. Again the cross-cultural perspective provides an invaluable corrective to the temptation to align aggression with power as distinguished from solidarity. Many cultures of the world see arguing as a pleasurable sign of intimacy. Schiffrin (1984) shows that among lower-middle-class men *and women* of East European Jewish background, friendly argument is a means of being sociable. Frank (1988) shows a Jewish couple who tend to polarize and take argumentative positions, but they are not fighting; they are staging a kind of public sparring, where both fighters are on the same team. Byrnes (1986) claims that Germans find American students uninformed and uncommitted because they are reluctant to argue politics with new acquaintances. For their part, Americans find German students belligerent because they provoke arguments about American foreign policy with Americans they have just met.

Greek conversation provides an example of a cultural style that places more positive value, for both women and men, on dynamic opposition. Kakava (1989) replicates Schiffrin's findings by showing how a Greek family enjoy opposing each other in dinner conversation. In another study of modern Greek conversation, Tannen and Kakava (1992) find speakers routinely disagreeing when they actually agree, and using diminutive name forms and other terms of endearment—markers of closeness—precisely when they are opposing each other.[13] These patterns can be seen in the following excerpt from a conversation that took place in Greece between an older Greek woman and myself. The woman, whom I call Ms. Stella, has just told me that she complained to the police about a construction crew that illegally continued drilling and pounding through the siesta hours, disturbing her nap:

> Deborah: Echete dikio.
>
> Stella: Ego <u>echo</u> dikio. Kopella mou, den xero an echo dikio i den echo dikio. Alla ego yperaspizomai ta symferonta mou kai ta dikaiomata mou.
>
> Deborah: You're right.
>
> Stella: I <u>am</u> right. My dear girl, I don't know if I'm right or I'm not right. But I am watching out for my interests and my rights.

My response to Ms. Stella's complaint is to support her by agreeing. But she disagrees with my agreement by reframing my statement in her own terms rather than simply accepting it by stopping after "I *am* right." She also marks her divergence from my frame with the endearment "kopella mou" (literally, "my girl," but idiomatically closer to "my dear girl").

The following conversation is also taken from Tannen and Kakava (1992). It is, according to Kakava, typical of her family's sociable argument. The younger sister has said that she cannot understand why the attractive young woman who is the prime minister Papandreou's girlfriend would have an affair with such an old man. The older sister, Christina, argues that the woman may have felt that in having an affair with the prime minister she was doing something notable. Her sister replied,

> Poly megalo timima re Christinaki na pliroseis pantos.
>
> It's a very high price to pay, Chrissie, anyway.

I use the English diminutive form "Chrissie" to reflect the Greek diminutive ending -*aki,* but the particle *re* cannot really be translated; it is simply a marker of closeness that is typically used when disagreeing, as in the ubiquitously heard expression "Ochi, re" ("No, *re*").

CONCLUSION

The intersection of language and gender provides a rich site for analyzing how power and solidarity are created in discourse. But prior research in this area evidences the danger of linking linguistic forms with interactional intentions such as dominance. In trying to understand how speakers use language, we must consider the context (in every sense, including at least textual, relational, and institutional constraints), speakers' conversational styles, and, most crucially, the interaction of their styles with each other.

Attempts to understand what goes on between women and men in conversation are muddled by the ambiguity and polysemy of power and solidarity. The same linguistic means can accomplish either, and every utterance combines elements of both. Scholars, however, like individuals in interaction, are likely to see only one and not the other, like the picture that cannot be seen for what it is—simultaneously a chalice and two faces—but can only be seen alternately as one or the other. In attempting the impossible task of keeping both images in focus at once, we may at least succeed in switching from one to the other rapidly and regularly enough to deepen our understanding of the dynamics underlying interaction such as power and solidarity as well as gender and language use.

NOTES

This chapter began as a paper entitled "Rethinking Power and Solidarity in Gender and Dominance," which was published in *Proceedings of the 16th Annual Meeting of the Berkeley Linguistics Society,* edited by Kira Hall, Jean-Pierre Koenig, Michael Meacham, Sondra Reinman, and Laurel A. Sutton, 519–29 (Berkeley: Linguistics Department, University of California, Berkeley, 1990). A significantly revised and expanded version appears in *Gender and Conversational Interaction,* a volume I edited, published by Oxford University Press in 1993. That rewriting was carried out while I was in residence at the Institute for Advanced Study in Princeton, New Jersey. Further revisions—improvements, I hope—which I made to the version that appears here (some in response to much-appreciated comments from Paul Friedrich) were carried out while I was a fellow at the Center for Advanced Study in the Behavioral Sciences in Palo Alto, California. I have lifted the summary of this chapter directly from the overview that appears in the 1993 publication.

1. I use the term "strategy" in its standard sociolinguistic sense, to refer simply to a way of speaking. No implication is intended of deliberate planning, as is the case in the common parlance use of such expressions as "military strategy." Neither, however, as Gumperz (1982) observes, are linguistic strategies "unconscious." Rather, they are best thought of as "automatic." That is, people speak in a particular way without "consciously" thinking it through, but are aware, if questioned, of how they spoke and what they were trying to accomplish by talking in that way. This is in contrast to the "unconscious" motives of Freudian theory about which an individual would be unaware if questioned. (For example, most men would vigorously deny that they want to kill their fathers and many their mothers, but a strict Freudian might claim that this wish is "unconscious.")

2. This example is taken from Tannen (1990).

3. I myself have made the observation that asymmetry is distancing whereas symmetry implies closeness, for example, with regard to the ritual of "troubles talk" and the way it often misfires between women and men (Tannen 1990). Many women talk about troubles as a way of feeling closer, but many men frequently interpret the description of troubles as a request for advice, which they kindly offer. I have observed that this not only cuts off the troubles talk, which was the

real point of the discourse, but it also introduces asymmetry: If one person says she has a problem and another says she has the same problem, they are symmetrically arrayed and their similarity brings them closer. But if one person has a problem and the other has the solution, the one with the solution is one-up, and the asymmetry is distancing—just the opposite of what was sought by initiating the ritual.

4. This assumption is made explicit by Klagsbrun (1992), who, in a book about sibling relationships, writes, "Unlike the ties between parents and children, the connection among siblings is a horizontal one. That is, sibs exist on the same plane, as peers, more or less equals" (12). But Klagsbrun gives a pivotal example of how she was frustrated as a child (and continues to be hampered, as an adult) by always being bested by her *older* brother. It is clear from the example that she and her brother were not equals because of the difference in their ages—and, one might argue, their genders.

5. Negative politeness, as discussed by Brown and Levinson ([1978]1987), entails honoring others' needs not to be imposed on.

6. Scollon (1982:344–45) explains that all communication is a double bind because one must serve, with every utterance, the conflicting needs to be left alone (negative face) and to be accepted as a member of society (positive face). The term "double bind" traces to Bateson (1972).

7. I have demonstrated at length (Tannen 1987, 1989) that repeating another's words creates rapport on a metalevel: It is a ratification of the other's words, evidence of participation in the same universe of discourse.

8. Following the oral presentation of this paper at the Berkeley Linguistics Society in 1989, both Gary Holland and Michael Chandler pointed out that the prisoner may be heard as implying the second part of the guard's statement: "and you're a pile of shit."

9. This scene illustrates what Bateson (1972) calls "complementary schismogenesis": Each person's style drives the other into increasingly exaggerated forms of the opposing behavior. The more he refuses to tell her what's wrong, the more desperate she becomes to break through his silence. The more she pressures him to tell her, the more adamant he becomes about refusing to do so.

10. Some examples are given in Tannen (1990). Whereas the boys made such gestures as shooting each other with invisible guns, the girls made such gestures as reaching out and adjusting a friend's headband.

11. Elsewhere (Tannen 1990:163–65) I discuss this example in more detail and note the contrast that the boys fight when they want to play, and the girl avoids disagreeing even when she in fact disagrees.

12. Another element of this epic, as Bly recounts it, is that Gilgamesh lures Enkidu away from the wild animals with which he had been happily living by

sending a temple prostitute who throws off her clothes at the appropriate moment. She is simply the vehicle for the two men to get together. Much could be said about this aspect of the epic, but my purpose here is only to draw attention to the way the men use fighting as a means to friendship.

13. Sifianou (1992) independently observes the use of diminutives as solidarity markers in Greek conversation.

REFERENCES

Bateson, Gregory. 1972. Steps to an ecology of mind. San Francisco: Chandler. Paperback: New York: Ballantine.

Becker, A. L. 1982. Beyond translation: Esthetics and language description. Contemporary perceptions of language: Interdisciplinary dimensions. Georgetown University Round Table on Languages and Linguistics 1982, ed. by Heidi Byrnes, 124–38. Washington, DC: Georgetown University Press.

Becker, A. L., and I Gusti Ngurah Oka. 1974. Person in Kawi: Exploration of an elementary semantic dimension. Oceanic Linguistics 13:229–55.

Beeman, William O. 1986. Language, status, and power in Iran. Bloomington: Indiana University Press.

Bellinger, David, and Jean Berko Gleason. 1982. Sex differences in parental directives to young children. Sex Roles 8:1123–39.

Bly, Robert. 1990. Iron John: A book about men. Reading, MA: Addison-Wesley.

Brown, Roger, and Albert Gilman. 1960. The pronouns of power and solidarity. Style in language, ed. by Thomas Sebeok, 253–76. Cambridge, MA: M.I.T. Press.

Brown, Penelope, and Stephen Levinson. [1978]1987. Politeness: Some universals in language usage. Cambridge: Cambridge University Press.

Byrnes, Heidi. 1986. Interactional style in German and American conversations. Text 6:2.189–206.

Campbell, Joseph. 1964. The masks of god: Occidental mythology. New York: Viking.

Coates, Jennifer. 1986. Women, men and language. London: Longman.

Conley, John M., William M. O'Barr, and E. Allen Lind. 1979. The power of language: Presentational style in the courtroom. Duke Law Journal 1978:1375–99.

Corsaro, William, and Thomas Rizzo. 1990. Disputes in the peer culture of American and Italian nursery school children. Conflict talk, ed. by Allen Grimshaw, 21–65. Cambridge: Cambridge University Press.

Dorval, Bruce (ed.). 1990. Conversational coherence and its development. Norwood, NJ: Ablex.

Duranti, Alessandro, and Donald Brenneis (eds.). 1986. The audience as coauthor. Special issue of Text 6:3.239–47.

Erickson, Frederick. 1986. Listening and speaking. Languages and linguistics: The interdependence of theory, data, and application. Georgetown University Round Table on Languages and Linguistics 1985, ed. by Deborah Tannen, 294–319. Washington, DC: Georgetown University Press.

Erickson, Frederick, and Jeffrey Shultz. 1982. The counselor as gatekeeper: Social interaction in interviews. New York: Academic Press.

Fasold, Ralph W. 1990. The sociolinguistics of language. Oxford: Basil Blackwell.

Frank, Jane. 1988. Communicating "by pairs": Agreeing and disagreeing among married couples. Unpublished ms., Georgetown University.

Friedrich, Paul. 1972. Social context and semantic feature: The Russian pronominal usage. Directions in sociolinguistics, ed. by John J. Gumperz and Dell Hymes, 270–300. New York: Holt, Rinehart, and Winston. Reprinted: Oxford: Basil Blackwell.

Gleason, Jean Berko. 1987. Sex differences in parent-child interaction. Language, gender, and sex in comparative perspective, ed. by Susan U. Philips, Susan Steele, and Christine Tanz, 189–99. Cambridge: Cambridge University Press.

Gumperz, John J. 1982. Discourse strategies. Cambridge: Cambridge University Press.

Hughes, Linda A. 1988. "But that's not *really* mean": Competing in a cooperative mode. Sex Roles 19:11/12.669–687.

James, Deborah, and Sandra Clarke. 1993. Women, men and interruptions: A critical review. Gender and conversational interaction, ed. by Deborah Tannen, 231–80. New York and Oxford: Oxford University Press.

James, Deborah, and Janice Drakich. 1993. Understanding gender differences in amount of talk. Gender and conversational interaction, ed. by Deborah Tannen, 281–312. New York and Oxford: Oxford University Press.

Jong, Erica. 1973. Fear of flying. New York: Holt, Rinehart and Winston.

Kakava, Christina. 1989. Argumentative conversation in a Greek family. Paper presented at the Annual Meeting of the Linguistic Society of America, Washington, DC.

Keenan, Elinor. 1974. Norm-makers, norm-breakers: Uses of speech by men and women in a Malagasy community. Explorations in the ethnography of speaking, ed. by Richard Bauman and Joel Sherzer, 125–43. Cambridge: Cambridge University Press.

Klagsbrun, Francine. 1992. Mixed feelings: Love, hate, rivalry, and reconciliation among brothers and sisters. New York: Bantam.

Komarovsky, Mirra. 1962. Blue-collar marriage. New York: Vintage.

Lakoff, Robin. 1975. Language and woman's place. New York: Harper and Row.

Maltz, Daniel N., and Ruth A. Borker. 1982. A cultural approach to male–female miscommunication. Language and social identity, ed. by John J. Gumperz, 196–216. Cambridge: Cambridge University Press.

McDermott, R. P., and Henry Tylbor. 1983. On the necessity of collusion in conversation. Text 3:3.277–97.

Mead, Margaret. 1977. End linkage: A tool for cross-cultural analysis. About Bateson, ed. by John Brockman, 171–231. New York: Dutton.

Norman, Michael. 1990. These good men: Friendships forged from war. New York: Crown.

Ong, Walter J. 1981. Fighting for life: Contest, sexuality, and consciousness. Ithaca, NY: Cornell University Press; Amherst: University of Massachusetts Press.

Paules, Greta Foff. 1991. Dishing it out: Power and resistance among waitresses in a New Jersey restaurant. Philadelphia: Temple University Press.

Philips, Susan Urmston. 1983. The invisible culture: Communication in classroom and community on the Warm Springs Indian reservation. New York and London: Longman. Reprinted: Prospect Heights, IL: Waveland Press.

Pinter, Harold. 1988. Mountain language. New York: Grove Press.

Sattel, Jack W. 1983. Men, inexpressiveness, and power. Language, gender and society, ed. by Barrie Thorne, Cheris Kramarae, and Nancy Henley, 119–24. Rowley, MA: Newbury House.

Schegloff, Emanuel. 1982. Discourse as an interactional achievement: Some uses of 'uhuh' and other things that come between sentences. Analyzing discourse: Text and talk. Georgetown University Round Table on Languages and Linguistics 1981, ed. by Deborah Tannen, 71–93. Washington, DC: Georgetown University Press.

Schegloff, Emanuel. 1988. Discourse as an interactional achievement II: An exercise in conversation analysis. Linguistics in context: Connecting observation and understanding, ed. by Deborah Tannen, 135–58. Norwood, NJ: Ablex.

Schiffrin, Deborah. 1984. Jewish argument as sociability. Language in Society 13:3.311–35.

Scollon, Ron. 1985. The machine stops: Silence in the metaphor of malfunction. Perspectives on silence, ed. by Deborah Tannen and Muriel Saville-Troike, 21–30. Norwood, NJ: Ablex.

Scollon, Ron, and Suzanne B. K. Scollon. 1981. Narrative, literacy and face in interethnic communication. Norwood, NJ: Ablex.

Shuy, Roger W. 1982. Topic as the unit of analysis in a criminal law case. Analyzing discourse: Text and talk. Georgetown University Round Table on Languages and Linguistics 1981, ed. by Deborah Tannen, 113–26. Washington, DC: Georgetown University Press.

Sifianou, Maria. 1992. The use of diminutives in expressing politeness: Modern Greek versus English. Journal of Pragmatics 17:2.155–73.

Spender, Dale. 1980. Man made language. London: Routledge and Kegan Paul.

Tannen, Deborah. 1981. Indirectness in discourse: Ethnicity as conversational style. Discourse Processes 4:3.221–38.

Tannen, Deborah. 1984. Conversational style: Analyzing talk among friends. Norwood, NJ: Ablex.

Tannen, Deborah. 1985. Silence: Anything but. Perspectives on silence, ed. by Deborah Tannen and Muriel Saville-Troike, 93–111. Norwood, NJ: Ablex.

Tannen, Deborah. 1986. That's not what I meant!: How conversational style makes or breaks your relations with others. New York: William Morrow. Paperback: Ballantine.

Tannen, Deborah. 1987. Repetition in conversation: Toward a poetics of talk. Language 63:3.574–605.

Tannen, Deborah. 1989. Talking voices: Repetition, dialogue and imagery in conversational discourse. Cambridge: Cambridge University Press.

Tannen, Deborah. 1990. You just don't understand: Women and men in conversation. New York: William Morrow. Paperback: Ballantine.

Tannen, Deborah, and Christina Kakava. 1992. Power and solidarity in Modern Greek conversation: Disagreeing to agree. Journal of Modern Greek Studies 10.12–29.

Watanabe, Suwako. 1993. Cultural differences in framing: American and Japanese group discussions, 176–208. Framing in discourse, ed. by Deborah Tannen. New York and Oxford: Oxford University Press.

Wolfowitz, Clare. 1991. Language style and social space: Stylistic choice in Suriname Javanese. Urbana and Chicago: University of Illinois Press.

West, Candace, and Don H. Zimmerman. 1983. Small insults: A study of interruptions in cross-sex conversations between unacquainted persons. Language, gender and society, ed. by Barrie Thorne, Cheris Kramarae, and Nancy Henley, 103–17. Rowley, MA: Newbury House.

Yamada, Haru. 1992. American and Japanese business discourse: A comparison of interactional styles. Norwood, NJ: Ablex.

CHAPTER TWO

Interpreting Interruption in Conversation

One of the discourse strategies discussed in chapter 1 is inter-ruption. Chapter 2 focuses entirely on this phenomenon. It draws on my research, spanning more than a dozen years, examining patterns and functions of overlap and interruption.

The phenomenon of interruption has been of focal interest to me for as long as I have been in the field of linguistics. My dissertation, later rewritten as Conversational Style: An-alyzing Talk Among Friends *(1984), examined a two-and-a-half-hour Thanksgiving dinner conversation between two Californians, three New York Jews, and a native of England. The study ended up being an analysis of what I called "high involvement style"—the conversational style of the New York Jewish speakers, of whom I was one. One of the most striking aspects of high involvement style that I found and analyzed in detail was the use of what I called "cooperative overlap": a listener talking along with a speaker not in order to interrupt but to show enthusiastic listenership and participation. The concept of overlap versus interruption became one of the corner-*

stones of my argument that the stereotype of New York Jews as pushy and aggressive is an unfortunate reflection of the effect of high involvement style in conversation with speakers who use a different style. (*In my study I called the other style "high considerateness"*).

This insight is the basis of my reluctance to jump on the "men dominate women by interrupting them" bandwagon. It is not that I deny that men often dominate women and that interruption is one way they often do so; however, my years of painstaking research into the workings of conversation have shown me that one cannot simply count overlaps in a conversation, call them interruptions, and assign blame to the speaker whose voice prevails.

In this chapter I address the theoretical issue of defining "interruption" in order to show that apparent interruption is not necessarily a display of dominance. The chapter is structured by the opening observation that the assumption that overlap is always interruption and that interruption perpetrates dominance has been questioned on methodological grounds, can be questioned on sociolinguistic grounds, and must be questioned on ethical grounds. I examine each of these objections in turn, juxtaposing research that finds men using interruption to dominate women with my own and others' research demonstrating that overlapping talk can be supportive rather than obstructive. Moreover, the conclusion that those who are observed to "interrupt" are intending to dominate, if applied to interactions among speakers of certain ethnic groups or among women, reinforces negative stereotyping of members of those groups—including women.

A JOKE HAS IT that a woman sues her husband for divorce. When the judge asks her why she wants a divorce, she explains that her husband has not spoken to her in two years. The judge then asks the husband, "Why haven't you spoken to your wife in two years?" He replies, "I didn't want to interrupt her."

This joke reflects the commonly held stereotype that women talk too much and interrupt men. On the other hand, one of the most widely cited findings to emerge from research on gender and language is that men interrupt women far more than women interrupt men. This finding is deeply satisfying insofar as it refutes the misogynistic stereotype and seems to account for the difficulty getting their voices heard that many women report having in interactions with men. At the same time, it reflects and bolsters common assumptions about the world: the belief that an interruption is a hostile act, with the interrupter an aggressor and the interrupted an innocent victim. Furthermore, it is founded on the premise that interruption is a means of social control, an exercise of power and dominance.

This research has been questioned on methodological grounds, can be questioned on sociolinguistic grounds, and must be questioned on ethical grounds, as it supports the stereotyping of a group of people on the basis of their conversational style. I here examine each of these objections in turn, juxtaposing the research that claims to find men interrupt women with my own and others' research on ethnicity and conversational style.

MALES INTERRUPT FEMALES: THE RESEARCH

Most widely cited for the finding that men interrupt women is the work of Candace West and Don Zimmerman (for example, Zimmerman and West 1975), West and Zimmerman 1983, 1985). This is not, however, the only research coming to the conclusion that males interrupt females. Others include Bohn and Stutman (1983), Eakins and Eakins (1976), Esposito (1979), Gleason and Greif (1983), and McMillan, Clifton, McGrath, and Gale (1977).[1]

Zimmerman and West (1975) recorded naturally occurring casual conversations on campus locations. They report that 96 percent of the interruptions they found (46 out of 48) were instances of men interrupting women. (The range is from no interruptions in one conversation to 13 in another). Following up with an experimentally designed study in which previously unacquainted first- and second-year undergraduates talked in cross-sex dyads, West and Zimmerman (1983) report a similar, though not as overwhelming, pattern: 75 percent of interruptions (21 of 28) were instances of men interrupting women.

Eakins and Eakins (1976) examined turn-taking patterns at seven faculty meetings and found that "men generally averaged a greater number of active interruptions per meeting than women, with eight being the highest average and two the lowest. For women the range was from two to zero" (58).

Some of the research finding that males interrupt females was carried out with children rather than adults. Esposito (1979:215) randomly assigned 40 preschool children to play groups and found that boys interrupted girls two to one. Examining the speech of 16 mothers and 16 fathers, Gleason and Greif (1983:147) found that fathers interrupt their children more than mothers, and that both interrupt female children more than male children.

INTERRUPTION AS DOMINANCE

West and Zimmerman (1983:103) are typical in calling interruption "a device for exercising power and control in conversation" and "violations of speakers' turns at talk." But they also claim that silence is a device for exercising dominance. They cite (108) Komarovsky (1962:353) to the effect that the "dominant" party in a marriage is often the more silent one, as revealed by the wife who says of her husband, "He doesn't say much but he means what he says and the children mind him." That men control and dominate women by refusing to speak is the main point of Sattel (1983), who illustrates with a scalding excerpt from Erica Jong's novel *Fear of Flying,* in which a wife becomes increasingly more desperate in her pleas for her husband to tell her what she has done to anger him. If both talking and not talking are dominating strategies, one wonders whether power and domination reside in the linguistic strategy at all or on some other level of interaction.

METHODOLOGICAL OBJECTION

All researchers who report that males interrupt females more than females interrupt males use mechanical definitions to identify interruptions. This is a function of their research goal: Counting requires coding, and coding requires "operational" definitions. For example, Zimmerman and West (1975), following Schegloff (1987),[2] define an interruption as a violation of the turn exchange system and an overlap as a misfire in it. If a second speaker begins speaking at what could be a transition-relevance place, it is counted as an overlap. The assumption is that the speaker mistook the potential transition-relevance place for an actual one. If a second speaker begins speaking at what could not be a transition-relevance place, it is counted as an interruption: The second speaker had evidence that the other speaker did not intend to relinquish a turn, but took the floor anyway, consequently trampling on the first speaker's right to continue speaking.

Most others who have studied this phenomenon have based their definitions on Zimmerman's and West's. For example, Esposito (1979) considered that "Interruptions occur when speaker A cuts off more than one word of speaker B's unit-type." Leffler, Gillespie, and Conaty (1982:156) did not distinguish between overlap and interruption. They included as interruptions "all vocalizations where, while one subject was speaking, the other subject uttered at least two consecutive identifiable words or at least three syllables of a single word." They eliminated, however, instances of repetition.

Operationally defined criteria, requisite and comforting to experimentally oriented researchers, are anathema to ethnographically oriented ones. Interruptions provide a paradigm case for such objections. Bennett (1981) points out that overlap and interruption are logically different types. (Barbara Johnstone [personal communication] suggests the linguistic terms "etic" and "emic" may serve here as well.) To identify overlap, one need only ascertain that two voices are going at once. (Overlap, then, is an "etic" category.) But to claim that a speaker interrupts another is an interpretive, not a descriptive act (an "emic" category). Whereas the term "overlap" is, in principle, neutral (though it also has some negative connotations), the label "interruption" is clearly negative. Affixing this label accuses a speaker of violating another speaker's right to the floor, of being a conversational bully. Claiming that one has "observed" an interruption is actually making a judgment, indeed what is generally perceived to be a moral judgment.

One of West's and Zimmerman's (1983:105) examples of interruption is a case of an overlap that seems justified in terms of interactional rights:

(1) Female: So uh you really can't bitch when you've got all those on
               the same day (4.2) but I uh asked my physics professor if
               I couldn't chan[ge that]
      Male: [Don't   ] touch that
               (1.2)
   Female: What?
               (#)
      Male: I've got everything jus'how I want it in that note-
               book (#) you'll screw it up leafin' through it like
               that.

This interruption is procedural rather than substantive. Many would argue that if the male feels that the female's handling of his note-book is destroying his organization of it, he has a right to ask her to desist immediately, without allowing further damage to be done while he awaits a transition-relevance place.[3]

Stephen Murray has mounted a number of attacks on Zimmerman and West on methodological grounds (Murray 1985, 1987; Murray and Covelli 1988). He argues, for example, that there can be no "absolute syntactical or acoustical criteria for recognizing an occurrence of 'interruption'" because a speaker's "completion rights" depend on a number of factors, including length or frequency of speech, number of points made, and special authority to speak on particular topics (Murray 1985). He also observes that whether or not a speaker feels interrupted is not absolute but varying by degree. He shows, for example, that the following interchange was judged an interruption by half the women he polled, but not by the other half:[4]

(2) H: I think [that

W: [Do you want some more salad?

Harvey Sacks observed that offering food often takes priority at a dinner table, and is heard not as an interruption but an aside. In this as in all matters of conversational rights and obligations, there are individual and cultural differences. Some people would feel interrupted if overlapped by an offer of salad; others would not. Many similar examples can be found of what might appear to be interruptions but are actually procedural metacomments that many consider rightful to override ongoing substantive talk.

SOCIOLINGUISTIC OBJECTION

Interpreting interruption as evidence of power or dominance assumes that interruption is a single-handed speech act, something one speaker does to another. But sociolinguistic research (for example, Duranti and Brenneis 1986; Erickson 1986; Goodwin 1981; McDermott and Tylbor 1983; Schegloff 1982, 1988) establishes that conversation is a joint production: Everything that happens is the doing of all participants. For an interruption to occur, two speakers must act: One must begin speaking, and another must stop. If the first speaker does not stop, there is no interruption. Thus even if an overlap is experienced as an interruption by a participant, it is wrongheaded for a researcher to conclude that the interruption is the doing of one party.

Furthermore, the contention that interruption is a sign of dominance reflects two assumptions that are neither universal nor obvious. One is that conversation is a fight for the floor. The validity of this contention varies with subcultural, cultural and individual predisposition as well as with the context of interaction. Yamada (1992), for example, argues that Japanese speakers prefer not to speak in potentially confrontational situations, since talk is seen as a liability. A similar view is attributed to Finns by Lehtonen and Sajavaara (1985).

Moreover, in light of the methodological objection that one cannot interpret the "meaning" of an overlap on the basis of its occurrence, many instances of overlap are supportive rather than obstructive. When students in one of my classes counted overlaps in half-hour casual conversations they had taped, the vast majority of overlaps, roughly 75 percent, were judged by the students who had taped the conversations to be cooperative rather than obstructive. Greenwood (1989) found that a high rate of interruption was a sign of social comfort in conversations among preadolescent boys and girls having dinner with their friends: The more comfortable the children reported feeling with their age-mate dinner guests, the more interruptions Greenwood observed in the transcript of their conversation.

Not only is it the case that a transcript might evidence overlap where participants did not feel that their speaking rights had been infringed upon, but participants might feel that their rights had been infringed upon where the transcript indicates they had not. For example, Greenwood discusses a segment in which Dara (age 12) and her sister Stephanie (age 11) have performed a humorous routine which climaxes with the utterance of a tongue twister for the benefit of their brother's dinner guest, Max (age 14). Although this routine sparked delighted laughter on other occasions among other friends, Max did not laugh and claimed not to get the joke. Dara and Stephanie try to explain it to him. Max recalls a tongue twister that he knows. When Dara and Stephanie continue their explanation, Max complains about being interrupted:

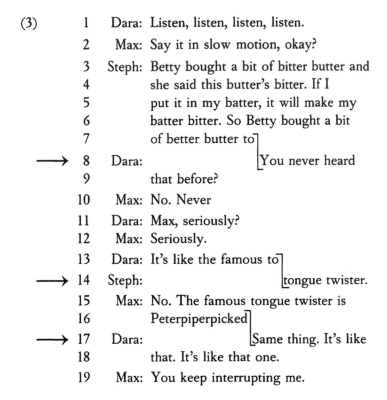

(3) 1 Dara: Listen, listen, listen, listen.

2 Max: Say it in slow motion, okay?

3 Steph: Betty bought a bit of bitter butter and
4 she said this butter's bitter. If I
5 put it in my batter, it will make my
6 batter bitter. So Betty bought a bit
7 of better butter to⌝

→ 8 Dara: ⌊You never heard
9 that before?

10 Max: No. Never

11 Dara: Max, seriously?

12 Max: Seriously.

13 Dara: It's like the famous to⌝

→ 14 Steph: ⌊tongue twister.

15 Max: No. The famous tongue twister is
16 Peterpiperpicked⌝

→ 17 Dara: ⌊Same thing. It's like
18 that. It's like that one.

19 Max: You keep interrupting me.

Though Dara and Stephanie repeatedly cut each other off, there is
no evidence that either resents the other's intrusions. Rather, they
are supporting each other, jointly performing one conversational
role—the common phenomenon that Falk (1980) calls a conversational duet. Though Max complains of being interrupted, the turn he
has taken in 15–16 ("No. The famous tongue twister is Peterpiper-
picked-") can easily be seen as an interruption of the girls' explanation, even though there is no overlap. In this interchange, the girls
are trying to include Max in their friendly banter, but by insisting on
his right to hold the floor without intrusions, he is refusing to be
part of their friendly group, rejecting their bid for solidarity. It
is therefore not surprising that Dara later told her mother that
she didn't like Max. Although Dara does "interrupt" Max at
17 to tell him he's got the idea ("Same thing. It's like that."),
there is no evidence that she is trying to dominate him. Further-

more, though Dara and Stephanie intrude into each other's turns, there is no evidence that they are trying to dominate each other either.

An assumption underlying the interruption-as-dominance paradigm is that conversation is an arrangement in which one speaker speaks at a time. Posited as an operational tenet by the earliest work on turntaking (Sacks, Schegloff and Jefferson 1974), this reflects ideology more than practice. Most Americans *believe* one speaker *ought* to speak at a time, regardless of what they actually do. I have played back to participants tape recordings of conversations that they had thoroughly enjoyed when they participated in them, in which many voices were heard at once, only to find that they are embarrassed upon hearing the recording, frequently acting as if they had been caught with their conversational pants down.

My own research demonstrates that simultaneous speech can be "cooperative overlapping"—that is, supportive rather than obstructive, evidence not of domination but of participation, not power, but the paradoxically related dimension, solidarity. Applying the framework that Gumperz (1982) developed for the analysis of crosscultural communication, I have shown apparent interruption to be the result of style contact—not the fault or intention of one party, but the effect of style differences in interaction.

In a two-and-a-half-hour Thanksgiving dinner conversation that I analyzed at length (Tannen 1984), interruptions resulted from conversants' differing styles with regard to pacing, pausing, and overlap. The conversation included many segments in which listeners talked along with speakers, *and the first speakers did not stop.* There was no interruption, only supportive, satisfying speaking together. For these speakers in this context, talking together was cooperative, showing understanding and participation. In the framework of politeness phenomena (Brown and Levinson 1987), overlaps were not perceived as violating speakers' negative face (their need not to be imposed on) but rather as honoring their positive face (their need to know that others are involved with them). It is an exercise not of power but of solidarity. The impression of dominance and interruption was not their intention, nor their doing. Neither, however, was it the creation of the imaginations of those who felt interrupted. It was the result of style contact, the interaction of two differing turn-taking systems.

I characterized the styles of the speakers who left little or no inter-turn pause, and frequently began speaking while another speaker was already speaking, as "high involvement" because the strategies of these speakers place relative priority on the need for positive face, to show involvement. When high involvement speakers used these (and other strategies I found to be characteristic of this style) with each other, conversation was not disrupted. Rather, the fast pacing and overlapping served to grease the conversational wheels. But when they used the same strategies with conversants who did not share this style, the interlocutors hesitated, faltered, or stopped, feeling interrupted and, more to the point, dominated. I characterized the style of these longer pause-favoring, overlap-aversant speakers as "high considerateness" because their strategies place relatively more emphasis on serving the need for negative face, not to impose.

I present here two examples to illustrate these two contrasting situations and the correspondingly contrasting effects of overlap on interaction. Example (4) shows overlapping that occurs in a segment of conversation among three high involvement speakers that has a positive effect on the interaction. Example (5) shows overlapping that occurs between high involvement and high considerateness speakers that results in mild disruption. Example (4) occurred in the context of a discussion about the impact of television on children. Steve's general statement that television has damaged chil dren sparks a question by Deborah (the author) about whether or not Steve and his brother Peter (who is also present) grew up with television:[5]

(4)	1	Steve:	I think it's basically done damage to
	2		children. .... That what good it's
	3		done is ... outweighed by ... the

5		damage.
6	Deborah:	Did you two grow up with
7		television?
8	Peter:	Very little. We had a TV in the
9		quonset
→ 10	Deborah:	How old were you when your parents got
11		it?
→ 12	Steve:	We had a TV but we didn't watch it
13		all the time. .... We were very young.
14		I was four when my parents got a
15		TV.
→ 16	Deborah:	You were four?
17	Peter:	I even remember that. ......
18		I don't remember /??/
→ 19	Steve:	I remember they got a TV before we
20		moved out of the quonset huts. In
21		1954.
→ 22	Peter:	I remember we got it in the
23		quonset huts.
24	Deborah:	[chuckle] You lived in quonset huts?
25		.... When you were how old?
		.....
26	Steve:	Yknow my father's dentist said to him
27		"What's a quonset hut." ... And he said
28		"God, you must be younger than my
29		children." .... He was. ....
30		Younger than both of us.

This interchange among three high involvement speakers evinces numerous overlaps and latchings (turn exchanges with no perceptible intervening pause). Yet the speakers show no evidence of discomfort. As the arrows indicate, all three speakers initiate turns that are latched onto or intruded into others' turns. Peter and Steve, who are brothers, operate as a duet, much as Dara and Stephanie did in (3).

Note, for example, lines 8–15: Peter's statement in 8 that begins "We had a TV in the quonset" is cut off by my question: 10 "How old were you when your parents got it?" Prior to answering my question, Steve repeats the beginning of his brother's sentence and completes it: 12 "We had a TV but we didn't watch it all the time." This statement blends smoothly into an answer to my question: 13–15 "We were very young. I was four when my parents got a TV." The change in focus from completing Peter's previous statement to answering my question can be seen in the change from first-person plural in "We had a TV" to first person singular in "I was four when my parents got a TV," as well as in the change in focus from the children having a TV (repeated from Peter's unfinished statement) to the parents getting it (repeated from my question). That Steve finished another thought (the one picked up from his brother) before answering my question, and the smoothness of the transition from one to the other, is evidence that he did not find the overlapped question intrusive.

A similar, even more striking example of the cooperative effect of overlapping in this example is seen in 26–30, where Steve ignores my question: 24–25 "You lived in quonset huts? When you were how old?" in favor of volunteering a vignette about his father that the reference to quonset huts has reminded him of. Part of the reason he does not find my questions intrusive is that he does not feel compelled to attend to them. Finally, the positive effect of overlapping in this interchange was supported by the participants' recollections during playback.

In (5) overlapping and latching were asymmetrical and unintentionally obstructive. David, an American Sign Language interpreter, is telling about ASL. As listeners, Peter and I used overlap and latching to ask supportive questions, just as I did in (4). (Note that the questions, in both examples, show interest in the speaker's discourse rather than shifting focus.)[6]

(5) 1   David: So: and this is the one that's
      2   Berkeley. This is the Berkeley ...
      3   sign for .. ⌈Christmas

→   4   Deborah: ⌊Do you figure out those ..
      5   those um correspondences? ⌈or do-
→   6   David: ⌊/?/
      7   when you learn the signs, /does/
      8   somebody tells you.

      9   David: Oh you mean ⌈watching it? like
→ 10   Deborah: ⌊Cause I can imagine
     11   knowing that sign, ... and not ..
     12   figuring out that it had anything to do
     13   with the decorations.
     14   ....

     15   David: No. Y- you know that it has to do with
     16   the decorations.⌉
→ 17   Deborah: ⌊'Cause somebody tells
     18   you? Or you figure ⌈it out.⌉
→ 19   David: ⌊No. ⌊Oh. ...
     20   You you talking about me,⌉or a deaf
     21   person.⌉
→ 22   Deborah: ⌊Yeah
     23   ⌊You. You.

     24   David: Me? Uh: Someone tells me, usually. ...
     25   But a lot of 'em I can tell. I mean
     26   they're obvious. .... The better I get
     27   the more I can tell. The longer I do
     28   it the more I can tell what they're
     29   talking about.⌈.....

     30   Deborah: ⌊Huh.
     31   Without ⌈knowing what the sign is.⌉

     32   Deborah: ⌊That's interesting.
     33   Peter: ⌊But

34		how do you learn a new sign?
		....
35	David:	How do I learn a new sign?
36	Peter:	⎡Yeah. I
37		mean supposing ... Victor's talking and
38		all of a sudden he uses a sign for
39		Thanksgiving, and you've never seen it
40		before.

In this interchange, all Peter's and my turns are latched or over-lapped on David's. In contrast, only two of David's seven turns overlap a prior turn; furthermore, these two utterances: an inaudible one at 6 and David's "No" at 19 are probably both attempts to answer the first parts of my double-barreled preceding turns (4–5 "Do you figure out those .. those um correspondences?" and 17 "'Cause somebody tells you?"). David shows evidence of discomfort in his pauses, hesitations, repetitions, and circumlocutions.

During playback, David averred that the fast pace of the questions, here and elsewhere, caught him off guard and made him feel borne in upon. It is difficult for me to regard this interchange in the merciless print of a transcript, because it makes me look overbearing. Yet I recall my good will toward David (who remains one of my closest friends) and my puzzlement at the vagueness of his answers. The comparative evidence of the other example, like numerous others in the dinner conversation, makes it clear that the fast-paced, latching, and overlapping questions (which I have dubbed "machine-gun questions") have exactly the effect I intended when used with co-stylists: They are taken as a show of interest and rapport; they encourage and reinforce the speaker. It is only in interaction with those who do not share a high involvement style that such questions and other instances of overlapping speech create disruptions and interruptions.

CULTURAL VARIATION

As Scollon (1985) argues, whenever interactants have different habits with regard to pacing, length of inter-turn pause, and attitudes toward simultaneous speech, unintended interruptions are inevitable because the speaker expecting a shorter pause perceives and fills an uncomfortable silence while the speaker expecting a longer pause is still awaiting a turn-signaling pause. This irritating phenomenon has serious consequences because the use of these linguistic strategies is culturally variable. It is no coincidence that the speakers in my study who had high involvement styles were of East European Jewish background and had grown up in New York City, whereas the speakers whose styles I have characterized as high considerateness were Christian and from California.

It is crucial to note that pacing, pausing, and attitude toward simultaneous speech have relative rather than absolute values. Characteristics such as "fast pacing" are not inherent values but result from the styles of speakers in interaction *relative to each other.* Whereas Californians in my study appeared to use relatively longer inter-turn pauses relative to the New Yorkers, Scollon and Scollon (1981) show that in conversations between midwestern Americans and Athabaskan Indians in Alaska, the Midwesterners become aggressive interrupters and Athabaskans their innocent victims, because the length of inter-turn pause expected by the midwesterners, while longer than that expected by Jewish New Yorkers, is significantly shorter than that expected by Athabaskans. In conversation with Scandinavians, most Americans become interrupters, but Swedes and Norwegians are perceived as interrupting by the longer pause-favoring and more silence-favoring Finns, who, according to Lehtonen and Sajavaara (1985), are themselves divided by internal regional differences with regard to length of pausing and pacing.

Labov and Fanshel (1977) claim that Rhoda, the 19-year-old psychotherapy patient in the therapeutic discourse they analyze, never ends her turn by falling silent. Rather, when she has said all she has to say, she begins to repeat herself, inviting the therapist to take a turn by overlapping her. This is an effective device for achieving smooth turn exchange without perceptible inter-turn silence, a high priority for speakers of a conversational style that sees silence in conversation, rather than simultaneous speech, as evidence of conversational trouble. It is not coincidental that the therapeutic interaction analyzed by Labov and Fanshel took place in New York City between Jewish speakers.

Reisman (1974) was one of the first to document a culturally recognizable style in which overlapping speech serves a cooperative rather than obstructive purpose. He coined the term "contrapuntal conversations" to describe this phenomenon in Antigua. Watson (1975) borrows this term to describe Hawaiian children's jointly produced verbal routines of joking and "talk story." As part of these routines, "turn-taking does not imply individual performance" but rather "partnership in performance" (55). Moerman (1988) makes similar observations about Thai conversation. Hayashi (1988) finds far more simultaneous speech among Japanese speakers than among Americans. Shultz, Florio, and Erickson (1982) find that an Italian-American boy who is reprimanded at school for unruly behavior is observing family conventions for turn-taking that include simultaneous speech.

Lein and Brenneis (1978) compared children's arguments in three speech communities: "white American children in a small town in New England, black American children of migrant harvesters, and rural, Hindi-speaking Fiji Indian children" (299). Although they found no overlaps in the arguments of the black American children and only occasional overlaps in the arguments of the white American children, the Fiji Indian children evidenced a great deal of overlap, continuing for as long as 30 seconds. Lein and Brenneis do not interpret these as misfires or errors but as "deliberate attempts to overwhelm the other speaker" (307). Although not cooperative in the sense of supportive, this use of sustained overlap is cooperative in the sense of playing by rather than breaking rules.[7]

Paradoxically (in light of the men-interrupt-women research), another group that has been described as favoring overlapping talk in in-group conversation is women. One of the first to make this observation was Kalčik (1975). Edelsky (1981), setting out to determine whether women or men talked more in a series of faculty committee meetings, found that she could not tackle this question without first confronting the question of the nature of a conversational floor. She found two types of floor: a singly developed floor in which one person spoke and the others listened silently, and a collaboratively developed floor in which more than one voice could be heard, to the extent that the conversation seemed, at times, like a "free-for-all." Edelsky found that men tended to talk more than women in singly developed floors, and women tended to talk as much as men in collaboratively developed floors.[8] In other words, this study implies that women are more comfortable talking when there is more than one voice going at once.

The following excerpt (6) shows women in casual conversation overlapping in a highly cooperative and collaborative interchange. It is taken from a naturally occurring conversation recorded by Janice Hornyak, that took place at a kitchen table.[9] Marge is visiting relatives in Washington, D.C., where her daughter Jan now lives, and is confronting snow for the first time. Peg and Marge, who are sisters-in-law, reminisce for Jan's benefit about the trials of having small children who like to play in the snow:

```
(6)        1     Peg:  The part I didn't like was putting
           2           everybody's snow pants and boots
           3          ⌈and
  ⟶       4     Marge:⌊Oh yeah that was the worst part,
           5      Peg:⌈and scarves
  ⟶       6     Marge:⌊and get them all bundled up in boots
           7           and everything and they're out for half
           8           an hour and then they come in and
           9           they're all covered with this snow and
          10           they get that schluck all over⌉
  ⟶      11     Peg:                                 ⌊All that
```

12		wet stuff and
→ 13	Jan:	That's why adults don't like snow, huh?
14	Marge:	That's right.
15	Peg:	Throw all the stuff in the dryer
16		and then they'd come in and sit for
17		half⌈an hour
→ 18	Marge:	⌊And in a little while they'd want
19		to go back out again.
20	Peg:	Then they want to go back out again.

As in the example of Steve, Peter, and me, all three speakers in this brief segment initiate turns that either latch onto or intrude into other speakers' turns. Like Dara and Stephanie in (3) and Steve and Peter in (4), Peg and Marge jointly hold one conversational role, overlapping without exhibiting (or reporting) resentment at being interrupted. Furthermore, Hornyak points out that these speakers often place the conjunction "and" at the end of their turns in order to create the appearance of overlap when there is none, as seen, for example, in 11–12 Peg: "All that wet stuff and".[10]

It is clear, then, that many, if not most, instances of overlap—at least in casual conversation among friends—have cooperative rather than obstructive effects. And even when the effect of overlap is perceived to be obstructive, the intent may still have been cooperative.

ETHICAL OBJECTION: STEREOTYPING AND CONVERSATIONAL STYLE

When people who are identified as culturally different have different conversational styles, their ways of speaking become the basis for negative stereotyping. Anti-Semitism classically attributes the characteristics of loudness, aggressiveness, and "pushiness" to Jewish speakers. The existence of this stereotype hardly needs support, but I provide a brief example that I recently encountered. In describing a Jewish fellow writer named Lowenfels, Lawrence Durrell wrote to Henry Miller, "He is undependable, erratic, has bad judgment, loud-mouthed, pushing, vulgar, thoroughly Jewish . . ." (Gornick 1988:47).

It is clear that the evaluation of Jews as loud and pushy simply blames the minority group for the effect of the interaction of differing styles.[11] Kochman (1981) demonstrates that a parallel style difference, which he calls the "rights of expressiveness" in contact with the "rights of sensibilities," underlies the stereotyping of community blacks as inconsiderate, overbearing, and loud. Finally, the model of conversation as an enterprise in which only one voice should be heard at a time is at the heart of misogynistic stereotypes as well. It is likely because of their use of cooperative overlapping in in-group talk that women are frequently stereotyped as noisily clucking hens.

GENDER, ETHNICITY, AND CONVERSATIONAL STYLE

The juxtaposition of these two lines of inquiry—gender and interruption, on the one hand, and ethnicity as conversational style on the other—poses a crucial and troubling dilemma. If it is theoretically wrongheaded, empirically indefensible, and morally insidious to claim that speakers of particular ethnic groups are pushy and dominating because they appear to interrupt in conversations with speakers of different, more "mainstream" ethnic backgrounds, can it be valid to embrace research which "proves" that men dominate women because they appear to interrupt them in conversation? If the researchers who have observed that men interrupt women in conversation were to "analyze" my audiotapes of conversations among New York Jewish and Christian Californian speakers, they would no doubt conclude that the New Yorkers "interrupted" and "dominated"—the impression of the Californians present, but not, I have demonstrated, the intention of the New Yorkers, nor the effect of their conversational styles in in-group interaction. My brief analysis here and extended analysis elsewhere (Tannen

1984) make clear that the use of overlapping speech by high involvement speakers does not create interruption in interaction with other similar-style speakers. In short, the "research" would do little more than apply the ethnocentric standards of the majority group to the culturally different behavior of the minority group.

The research on gender and interruption presents a sociolinguistic parallel but a political contrast. Although not a minority, women are at a social and cultural disadvantage. This transforms the political consequences of blaming one group for dominating the other. Most people would agree that men dominate women in our culture, as in most if not all cultures of the world. Therefore many would claim (as do Henley and Kramarae 1988) that sociolinguists like Maltz and Borker (1982) and me (Tannen 1986) who view gender differences in conversation in the framework of Gumperz's (1982) paradigm for cross-cultural communication, are simply copping out—covering up real domination with a cloth of cultural difference. Though I am sympathetic to this view, my conscience tells me we cannot have it both ways. If we accept the research in one paradigm—the men-interrupt-women one—then we are forced into a position that claims that high involvement speakers, such as blacks and Jews and, in many circumstances, women, are pushy, aggressive, or inconsiderately or foolishly noisy.

Finally, given the interaction among gender, ethnicity, and conversational style, what are the consequences for American women of ethnic backgrounds characterized by high involvement conversational styles—styles perceived by other Americans as pushy, aggressive, and dominating? The view of conversational style as power from the men-interrupt-women paradigm yields the repugnant conclusion that many women (including many of us of African, Caribbean, Mediterranean, South American, Levantine, Arab, and East European backgrounds) are dominating, aggressive, and pushy—qualities, moreover, that are perceived as far more negative in women than in men. It was just such a standard that led Barbara Bush to label Geraldine Ferraro "the word that rhymes with rich" when Ferraro spoke in ways accepted, indeed expected, in male politicians.

CONCLUSION

As a woman who has personally experienced the difficulty many women report in getting heard in some interactions with men, I am tempted to embrace the studies that find that men interrupt women: It would allow me to explain my experience in a way that blames others. As a high involvement style speaker, however, I am offended by the labeling of a feature of my conversational style as loathsome, based on the standard of those who do not share or understand it. As a Jewish woman raised in New York who is not only offended but frightened by the negative stereotyping of New Yorkers and women and Jews, I recoil when scholarly research serves to support the stereotyping of a group of speakers as possessing negative intentions and character. As a linguist and researcher, I know that the workings of conversation are more complex than that. As a human being, I want to understand what is really going on. Such understanding, I conclude, remains to be delivered by discourse analysts concerned with investigating patterns of turn-taking in conversation.

AFTERWORD

My Chicago Linguistic Society paper (see unnumbered note) ends here, but the chapter entitled "Who's Interrupting? Issues of Dominance and Control" in *You Just Don't Understand: Women and Men in Conversation* continues. Importantly, it includes two more examples taken from a short story entitled "You're Ugly, Too" by Lorrie Moore (1989), in which overlapping is not cooperative. In one example a man takes the floor from a woman by taking over the telling of a joke that she has already begun to tell. In the other, he changes the subject after she has announced her intention to tell a story. I added those examples to avoid the false impression that my intention was to deny that interruption exists, that overlap can be intended to interrupt, or that men can use interruption to silence women.

Since these examples are taken from literature rather than life, their status is somewhat different from that of excerpts from conversational transcripts. They are intended as illustrations of a type of interruption that can occur, not as proof that such interruption does occur, although I do not doubt that it does. The relevant passages are reproduced here. Whereas women's cooperative overlaps frequently annoy men by seeming to co-opt their topic, men frequently annoy women by usurping or switching the topic. An example of this kind of interruption is portrayed in "You're Ugly, Too," a short story by Lorrie Moore. The heroine of this story, Zoë, a history professor, has had an ultrasound scan to identify a growth in her abdomen. Driving home after the test, she looks at herself in the rear-view mirror and recalls a joke:

> She thought of the joke about the guy who visits his doctor and the doctor says, "Well, I'm sorry to say, you've got six weeks to live."
> "I want a second opinion," says the guy. . . .
> "You want a second opinion? OK," says the doctor. "You're ugly, too." She liked that joke. She thought it was terribly, terribly funny. (77)

Later in the story, at a Halloween party, Zoë is talking to a recently divorced man named Earl whom her sister has fixed her up with. Earl asks, "What's your favorite joke?" This is what happens next:

> "Uh, my favorite joke is probably . . . OK, all right. This guy goes into a doctor's office, and—"
> "I think I know this one," interrupted Earl, eagerly. He wanted to tell it himself. "A guy goes into a doctor's office, and the doctor tells him he'g got some good news and some bad news—that one, right?"
> "I'm not sure," said Zoë. "This might be a different version."

75

"So the guy says, 'Give me the bad news first,' and the doctor says, 'OK. You've got three weeks to live.' And the guy cries, 'Three weeks to live! Doctor, what is the good news?' And the doctor says, 'Did you see that secretary out front? I finally fucked her.'"

Zoë frowned.

"That's not the one you were thinking of?"

"No." There was accusation in her voice. "Mine was different."

"Oh," said Earl. He looked away and then back again. "You teach history, right? What kind of history do you teach?"

(84)

When Earl interrupts Zoë, it is not to support her joke but to tell her joke for her. (To make matters worse, the joke he tells isn't just different; it's offensive.) When he finds out that his joke was not the same as hers, he doesn't ask her what hers was. Instead, he raises another topic entirely ("What kind of history do you teach?").

Most people would agree that Earl's interruption violates Zoë's speaking rights, because it came as Zoë was about to tell a joke and usurped the role of joke-teller. But note that Zoë yielded quickly to Earl's bid to tell her joke. As soon as he said, "some good news and some bad news," it was obvious that he had a different joke in mind, but instead of answering "No" to his question, "that one, right?" Zoë said, "I'm not sure. This might be a different version," supporting his bid and allowing for agreement where there really was disagreement. Someone who viewed conversation as a contest could have taken back the floor at this point, if not before. But Zoë seems to view conversation as a game requiring each speaker to support the other's words. It may be that Earl (or his real-life model) would have preferred if she had competed for the right to tell the joke instead of letting him go on when he hadn't really gotten it right.

Another part of the same story shows that it is not overlap that creates interruption but conversational moves that wrench a topic away from another speaker's course. Zoë feels a pain in her stomach and excuses herself and disappears into the bathroom. When she returns, Earl asks if she's all right, and she tells him that she has been having medical tests. Rather than asking her about them, Earl gives her some food that had been passed around while she was in the bathroom. Chewing the food, she says, "With my luck, it'll be a gallbladder operation." Earl changes the subject: "So your sister's getting married? Tell me, really, what you think about love." Zoë begins to answer:

> "All right. I'll tell you what I think about love. Here is a love story. This friend of mine—
> "You've got something on your chin," said Earl, and he reached over to touch it. (89)

Although, like offering food, taking something off someone's face may take priority over talk, doing so just when she has started to tell a story seems like a sign of lack of interest in her story, and lack of respect for her right to continue it. Furthermore, this is not an isolated incident, but one in a series. Earl did not follow up Zoë's self-revelation about her health with questions or support, didn't offer advice, and didn't match her revelation with a mutual one about himself. Instead, he shifted the conversation to another topic—love—which he might have felt was more appropriate than a gallbladder operation for initiating a romantic involvement. (For the same reason, taking something off her chin may have been too good an opportunity for touching her face to pass up. Indeed, many of his moves seem to be attempts to steer the conversation in the direction of flirtation.)

NOTES

I presented the material included in this chapter in 1989 as an invited speaker at the 25th Annual Regional Meeting of the Chicago Linguistic Society. The paper appears, almost exactly as it appears here, in the volume by the same name: *Papers from the 25th Annual Regional Meeting of the Chicago Linguistic Society. Part Two:*

Parasession on Language in Context, ed. by Bradley Music, Randolph Graczyk, and Caroline Wiltshire, 266–87. Chicago: Chicago Linguistic Society. I have made only a few very minor changes and updated the references. This paper also provided the basis for a chapter entitled "Who's Interrupting? Issues of Dominance and Control" in *You Just Don't Understand: Women and Men in Conversation.* In developing the material for that book, I not only rewrote the paper in a style comprehensible to nonspecialists but also eliminated some parts of the argument and added others, including the part that appears as an afterword to the present chapter.

1. See James and Clarke (1993) for a critical review of the literature on gender and interruption.

2. Schegloff takes issue with Zimmerman's and West's imposition of gender as a category on transcripts in which there is no evidence that the participants' gender is a live issue. He does not, however, take issue with their definition and identification of interruptions.

3. There are other aspects of this excerpt that lead one to conclude this male speaker may be a conversational bully, other than the fact of interrupting to protect his property.

4. In the original publication of this chapter as well as in *You Just Don't Understand: Women and Men in Conversation* I present this as Murray's example of a "prototypical" interruption. He has since corrected me, pointing out that he had noted that interpretations of this example vary.

5. Overlapping is shown by brackets; brackets with reverse flaps show latching. Two dots (. .) indicate perceptible pause of less than a half second. Three dots indicate a half-second pause; each extra dot indicates an additional half second of pause. /?/ indicates indecipherable utterance. All the questions in (4) are spoken with fast pace and high pitch. Quonset huts were temporary housing structures provided by the American government for returning veterans following World War II.

6. The question was posed whether David's discomfort was caused by his role as spokesperson for ASL. Although this may have exacerbated it, the pattern of hesitation exhibited in this excerpt is typical of many involving David and another participant, Chad, as shown in the longer study (Tannen 1984) from which these brief examples are taken.

7. It cannot be assumed that apparent conflict is necessarily truly agonistic. Corsaro and Rizzo (1990), for example, demonstrate that children in an Italian nursery school deliberately provoke highly ritualized, noisy disputes when they are supposed to be quietly drawing because, as the authors put it, they would rather fight than draw. Schiffrin (1984) demonstrates that apparent argument serves a sociable purpose among working-class Jewish speakers in Philadelphia.

8. Edelsky notes that her initial impression had been that women "dominated" in the collaboratively developed floors, but closer observation revealed they had not. This supports the frequently heard claim (for example Spender 1980) that when women talk as much as men they are perceived as talking more.

9. Hornyak recorded and analyzed this excerpt as part of her coursework in my discourse analysis class, spring 1989. I thank her for her data, her insights, and her permission to use them here.

10. Hornyak claims this is a family strategy which is satisfying and effective when used among family members but is often the object of complaint by non-family members when used with them. Though she thinks of this as a family strategy, I wonder whether it might not be a cultural one. The family is of Hungarian descent, and evidence abounds that cooperative overlapping is characteristic of many East European speakers.

11. No group is homogeneous; any attempt to characterize all members of a group breaks down on closer inspection. The high involvement style I refer to here is not so much Jewish as East European. German Jews do not typically exhibit such style, and of course many American Jews have either abandoned, modified, or never acquired high involvement styles.

REFERENCES

Bennett, Adrian. 1981. Interruptions and the interpretation of conversation. Discourse Processes 4:2.171–88.

Brown, Penelope, and Stephen C. Levinson. 1987. Politeness: Some universals in language usage. Cambridge: Cambridge University Press.

Bohn, Emil, and Randall Stutman. 1983. Sex-role differences in the relational control dimension of dyadic interaction. Women's Studies in Communication 6.96–104.

Corsaro, William, and Thomas Rizzo. 1990. Disputes in the peer culture of American and Italian nursery school children. Conflict talk, ed. by Allen Grimshaw, 21–66. Cambridge: Cambridge University Press.

Duranti, Alessandro, and Donald Brenneis (eds.). 1986. The audience as co-author. Special issue of Text 6:3.239–47.

Eakins, Barbara, and Gene Eakins. 1976. Verbal turn-taking and exchanges in faculty dialogue. The sociology of the languages of American women, ed. by Betty Lou Dubois and Isabel Crouch, 53–62. Papers in Southwest English IV. San Antonio, TX: Trinity University.

Edelsky, Carol. 1981. Who's got the floor? Language in Society 10.383–421. Reprinted in Gender and conversational interaction, ed. by Deborah Tannen, 189–227. Oxford and New York: Oxford University Press, 1993.

Erickson, Frederick. 1986. Listening and speaking. Languages and linguistics: The interdependence of theory, data, and application. Georgetown University Round Table on Languages and Linguistics 1985, ed. by Deborah Tannen, 294–319. Washington, DC: Georgetown University Press.

Esposito, Anita. 1979. Sex differences in children's conversations. Language and Speech 22, Pt. 3, 213–20.

Falk, Jane. 1980. The conversational duet. Proceedings of the Sixth Annual Meeting of the Berkeley Linguistics Society, 507–14. Berkeley, CA: University of California.

Gleason, Jean Berko, and Esther Blank Greif. 1983. Men's speech to young children. Language, gender and society, ed. by Barrie Thorne, Cheris Kramarae, and Nancy Henley, 140–50. Rowley, MA: Newbury House.

Goodwin, Charles. 1981. Conversational organization: Interaction between speakers and hearers. New York: Academic Press.

Gornick, Vivian. 1988. Masters of self-deception. Review of *The Durrell-Miller letters, 1935–80*, ed. by Ian S. MacNiven. The New York Times Book Review, November 20, 1988, 3, 47.

Greenwood, Alice. 1989. Discourse variation and social comfort: A study of topic initiation and interruption patterns in the dinner conversation of pre-adolescent children. Ph.D. dissertation, City University of New York.

Gumperz, John J. 1982. Discourse strategies. Cambridge: Cambridge University Press.

Hayashi, Reiko. 1988. Simultaneous talk—from the perspective of floor management of English and Japanese speakers. World Englishes 7:3.269–88.

Henley, Nancy, and Cheris Kramarae. 1988. Miscommunication—Issues of gender and power. Paper presented at the annual meeting of the National Women's Studies Association, Minneapolis.

James, Deborah, and Sandra Clarke. 1993. Women, men and interruptions: A critical review. Gender and conversational interaction, ed. by Deborah Tannen, 231–80. New York and Oxford: Oxford University Press.

Kalčik, Susan. 1975. ". . . like Ann's gynecologist or the time I was almost raped": Personal narratives in women's rap groups. Journal of American Folklore 88:3–11. Reprinted in Women and folklore, ed. by Claire R. Farrer, 3–11. Austin: University of Texas Press, 1975.

Kochman, Thomas. 1981. Black and white styles in conflict. Chicago: University of Chicago Press.

Komarovsky, Mirra. 1962. Blue-collar marriage. New York: Vintage.

Labov, William, and David Fanshel. 1977. Therapeutic discourse. New York: Academic Press.

Leffler, Ann, D. L. Gillespie, and J. C. Conaty. 1982. The effects of status differentiation on nonverbal behavior. Social Psychology Quarterly 45:3.153–61.

Lehtonen, Jaakko, and Kari Sajavaara. 1985. The silent Finn. Perspectives on silence, ed. by Deborah Tannen and Muriel Saville-Troike, 193–201. Norwood, NJ: Ablex.

Lein, Laura, and Donald Brenneis. 1978. Children's disputes in three speech communities. Language in Society 7.299–323.

Maltz, Daniel N., and Ruth A. Borker. 1982. A cultural approach to male–female miscommunication. Language and social identity, ed. by John J. Gumperz, 196–216. Cambridge: Cambridge University Press.

McDermott, R. P., and Henry Tylbor. 1983. On the necessity of collusion in conversation. Text 3:3.277–97.

McMillan, Julie R., A. Kay Clifton, Diane McGrath, and Wanda S. Gale. 1977. Women's language: Uncertainty or interpersonal sensitivity and emotionality. Sex Roles 3:6.545–59.

Moerman, Michael. 1988. Talking culture: Ethnography and conversation analysis. Philadelphia: University of Pennsylvania Press.

Moore, Lorrie. 1989. You're ugly, too. The New Yorker, July 3, 1989, 34–40. Reprinted in *Like life.* New York: Alfred A. Knopf, 1990.

Murray, Stephen O. 1985. Toward a model of members' methods for recognizing interruptions. Language in Society 13:31–41.

Murray, Stephen O. 1987. Power and solidarity in "interruption": A critique of the Santa Barbara School conception and its application by Orcutt and Harvey (1985). Symbolic Interaction 10:1.101–10.

Murray, Stephen O., and Lucille H. Covelli. 1988. Women and men speaking at the same time. Journal of Pragmatics 12:1.103–11.

Reisman, Karl. 1974. Contrapuntal conversations in an Antiguan village. Explorations in the ethnography of speaking, ed. by Richard Bauman and Joel Sherzer, 110–24. Cambridge: Cambridge University Press.

Sacks, Harvey, Emanuel Schegloff, and Gail Jefferson. 1974. A simplest systematics for the organization of turn-taking for conversation. Language 50:696–735.

Sattel, Jack W. 1983. Men, inexpressiveness, and power. Language, gender and society, ed. by Barrie Thorne, Cheris Kramarae, and Nancy Henley, 119–24. Rowley, MA: Newbury House.

Schegloff, Emanuel. 1982. Discourse as an interactional achievement: Some uses of 'uhuh' and other things that come between sentences. Analyzing discourse: Text and talk. Georgetown University Round Table on Languages and Linguistics 1981, ed. by Deborah Tannen, 71–93. Washington, DC: Georgetown University Press.

Schegloff, Emanuel. 1987. Between micro and macro: Contexts and other connections. The micro–macro link, ed. by Jeffrey C. Alexander, Bernhard Giesen, Richard Munch, and Neil J. Smelser, 207–34. Berkeley: University of California Press.

Schegloff, Emanuel. 1988. Discourse as an interactional achievement II: An exercise in conversation analysis. Linguistics in context: Connecting observation and understanding, ed. by Deborah Tannen, 135–58. Norwood, NJ: Ablex.

Schiffrin, Deborah. 1984. Jewish argument as sociability. Language in Society 13:3.311–35.

Scollon, Ron. 1985. The machine stops: Silence in the metaphor of malfunction. Perspectives on silence, ed. by Deborah Tannen and Muriel Saville-Troike, 21–30. Norwood, NJ: Ablex.

Scollon, Ron, and Suzanne, B. K. Scollon. 1981. Narrative, literacy and face in interethnic communication. Norwood, NJ: Ablex.

Shultz, Jeffrey, Susan Florio, and Frederick Erickson. 1982. Where's the floor? Aspects of the cultural organization of social relationships in communication at home and at school. Ethnography and education: Children in and out of school, ed. by Perry Gilmore and Alan Glatthorn, 88–123. Washington, DC: Center for Applied Linguistics (distributed by Ablex).

Spender, Dale. 1980. Man made language. London: Routledge and Kegan Paul.

Tannen, Deborah. 1981. New York Jewish conversational style. International Journal of the Sociology of Language 30.133–39.

Tannen, Deborah. 1984. Conversational style: Analyzing talk among friends. Norwood, NJ: Ablex.

Tannen, Deborah. 1986. That's not what I meant!: How conversational style makes or breaks your relations with others. New York: William Morrow. Paperback: New York: Ballantine.

Watson, Karen A. 1975. Transferable communicative routines. Language in Society 4:53–72.

West, Candace, and Don H. Zimmerman. 1983. Small insults: A study of interruptions in cross-sex conversations between unacquainted persons. Language, gender and society, ed. by Barrie Thorne, Cheris Kramarae, and Nancy Henley, 103–17. Rowley, MA: Newbury House.

West, Candace, and Don. H. Zimmerman. 1985. Gender, language, and discourse. Handbook of discourse analysis, Vol. 4, Discourse analysis in society, ed. by Teun A. van Dijk, 103–24. London: Academic Press.

Yamada, Haru. 1992. American and Japanese business discourse: A comparison of interactional styles. Norwood, NJ: Ablex.

Zimmerman, Don H., and Candace West. 1975. Sex roles, interruptions and silences in conversation. Language and sex: Difference and dominance, ed. by Barrie Thorne and Nancy Henley, 105–29. Rowley, Mass.: Newbury House.

CHAPTER THREE

Gender Differences in Conversational Coherence

Physical Alignment and Topical Cohesion

This chapter reports a study I conducted of children talking to their best friends across four ages, from second graders to adults. The chapter begins with a brief introduction to the cross-cultural approach to gender differences in conversation. Then it compares the 20-minute conversations of four pairs each of male and female best friends. I found that at every age the girls and women in the study oriented to each other with their bodily alignment and gazed at each other more directly than did the boys and men. The females at each age quickly established topics for talk and produced extended talk about a small number of topics. In contrast, the second- and sixth-grade boys produced small amounts of talk about many different topics. Tenth-grade boys and graduate-school age men produced a lot of talk about a few topics, but the level at which they discussed the topics was more abstract, and their discussion of personal problems was more indirect. Thus the analysis contradicts the frequently heard claim that women's language is more indirect than men's. In this context, both physical

*alignment and topical cohesion are more tightly or directly
focused in the females' talk. I argue, however, that the male
style is equally engaged. The boys' physical alignment, in
particular that of the tenth graders, provides a metaphor for
understanding the coherence in the boys' and men's dialogue:
their engagement proceeds as if on parallel tracks.*

INTRODUCTION

I N INTRODUCING A collection of essays entitled *Coherence in
Spoken and Written Discourse,* I defined *coherence* as "underlying
organizing structure making the words and sentences into a unified
discourse that has cultural significance for those who create or com-
prehend it," as distinct from *cohesion,* which I defined as "surface-
level ties showing relationships among elements in the text" (Tannen 1984, p. xiv). These definitions now strike me as too static,
perhaps more applicable to monologic discourse than to the interactive discourse of conversation. The organization of coherence in
conversation must be not a preexisting structure, but an emergent
one, much as Hopper (1988) shows grammar to be emergent. In
other words, conversation is not like flesh shaped by a preformed
skeleton, but a shape which is renegotiated in interaction, created
anew by participants in accordance with shared expectations based
on previous conversational experience, or what Becker (1988) calls
"prior text."

Two elements of emergent coherence in conversation—that is,
two elements that create an integrated activity, conversation, out of
individuals' separate speech—are physical alignment and topical
cohesion. By *physical alignment* I mean the ways that speakers position their heads and bodies in relation to each other, including eye
gaze. With Schiffrin (1988), I take "topic" to be, simply, "what
speakers talk about." *Topical cohesion* then refers to how speakers
introduce and develop topics in relation to their own and others'
prior and projected talk. This chapter describes and discusses physi-

cal alignment and topical cohesion in 20-minute videotapes of eight pairs of friends, one female and one male pair at each of four age levels: second graders, sixth graders, tenth graders, and 25-year-olds.[1]

The videotapes were made by Bruce Dorval, who visited second-, sixth-, and tenth-grade classrooms and invited students to come to his office on a university campus and talk to their same-sex best friends for 20 minutes. He left them alone for the duration of the conversations, which were videotaped by a stationary video recorder in the office. He also invited adult women and men who attended his psychology courses at the university to bring their best friends to his office for the same purpose. To begin the conversations, he instructed each pair of friends to find "something serious and/or intimate" to talk about, and he informed them that he would be returning in 5 minutes to remind them of these instructions.[2]

In 1986, Dorval organized a study group, with support from the Society for Research in Child Development, to which he invited scholars in a range of disciplines to examine the videotapes. As one of those invited, I did not approach these data with the intention of examining gender differences. Rather, I intended to analyze involvement strategies such as repetition and dialogue, in keeping with the focus of my current research (Tannen 1987, 1988, 1989). However, watching the videotapes of same-sex pairs at each age level, I was so struck by gender-related patterns that I could not resist the drive to study them more closely. My own previous research includes only one study of gender differences, specifically, of indirectness in conversation (see chapter 5). But for a general book about conversational style (Tannen 1986a), I had reviewed and discussed recent research on gender differences. Some of the patterns I observed in the videotapes of friends talking supported previous studies of which I was aware, but some were unexpected to me. Inspired, in part, by the striking impression made by these data, I decided to devote a book to gender differences in conversational style (Tannen 1990).

Overview of gender-related patterns in the videotapes. Watching the videotapes of the boys and girls and women and men at these four age levels, I observed that there were patterns which linked the speakers of like gender across the ages and distinguished cross-gender age-mates. At every age level, the girls and women oriented to each other with the alignment of their bodies and gaze far more directly than did the boys and men. Whereas all the pairs displayed discomfort with the experimental situation and the assigned task, at every age level, the female friends quickly established topics for talk and produced extended talk related to a small number of topics. In contrast, boys at the two younger ages produced small amounts of talk about many different topics. At the two older ages, the boys and men, like their female counterparts, produced a lot of talk about a few topics, but the level at which they discussed the topics was more abstract, less personal.

A cross-cultural view of gender differences. Despite these findings of gender differences, I question the conclusion made by researchers in the field of family therapy as well as by women who interact with men in everyday life that, because the boys and men are less directly aligned with their interlocutors in posture and gaze, they are not "engaged" or "involved." Furthermore, I question the conclusion that, because the boys produce small amounts of talk about each of a large number of topics, they are evidencing a failure or lack. Rather, I subscribe to a cross-cultural approach to cross-gender conversation by which women and men, boys and girls, can be seen to accomplish and display coherence in conversation in different but equally valid ways.

A model for understanding cross-cultural communication is provided by Gumperz (1982). That such an approach can be applied to conversations between women and men is demonstrated by Maltz and Borker (1982), on the basis of ethnographic research on language socialization by sociologists and anthropologists, especially the work of Goodwin (1990) and others. Only a brief summary can be provided here.

Based on microanalysis of conversations among British speakers of English and speakers of English from India and Pakistan in London, as well as among black and white speakers of English in the United States, Gumperz demonstrates that interlocutors accomplish conversational inferencing and identify the speech activity they are engaged in by means of contextualization cues: aspects of talk such as intonation, prosody, loudness, pitch, sequencing, and choice of words, that both signal and create the context in which communication is taking place. But speakers of different cultural backgrounds use different contextualization cues. In other words, they have different habits for contextualizing their talk: different ways of signalling similar speech activities. In cross-cultural communication, such cues, therefore, are likely to be misinterpreted or missed altogether.

Reviewing the work of Goodwin and others, Maltz and Borker (1982) explain that males and females learn their styles of talking in sex-separate peer groups. In this sense, they grow up in different cultural environments, so they too develop different habits for signalling their intentions and understandings. Because they learn to have conversations in same-sex peer interaction, women and men develop different norms for establishing and displaying conversational involvement. These "cultural" differences account for the differing patterns observed among girls and boys and women and men, as well as for mutual negative evaluations that often result from cross-gender interactions.

In the discussion that follows I consider patterns of physical alignment first and then move to topical cohesion.

PHYSICAL ALIGNMENT

Overview. Patterns of physical alignment which link same-gender speakers in all the videotapes studied, and differentiate pairs of speakers of different genders at similar age levels, can be instantly appreciated by watching the videotapes with the sound turned off. Even if there were no differences in how they spoke, their physical alignment, body posture, movements, and eye gaze make for very different forms of conversational involvement.

At each of the four age levels, the girls and women sit closer to each other. They sit across the chairs in order to align their bodies facing each other. They anchor their gaze on each other's faces with occasional glances away. They also occasionally touch each other, and they sit relatively still. In contrast, at every age level, the boys and men are less directly aligned with each other in terms of body posture and gaze. Their chairs are at angles to each other, and they sit aligned with the chairs and, consequently, at angles to each other. They anchor their gaze elsewhere in the room, occasionally glancing at each other, rarely if ever head on. The two younger pairs of boys are restless and seemingly diffuse in their attention; they give the impression that the chairs cannot contain them. The two older male pairs sit still but align themselves more or less parallel rather than facing each other. The tenth-grade boys in particular sprawl out from the chairs rather than sitting in them.[3]

In this section, I proceed by age level to describe the physical alignment of the boys and girls or men and women, in comparison to each other at each level.

Grade two. The second-grade boys, Kevin and Jimmy, look at each other only occasionally. (See figure 3.1.) They look around the room, look at the ceiling, squirm in their chairs, get up and sit down again, pummel the arms of the chair (the one whose chair has arms), rhythmically kick their feet, make faces, point to objects in the room, mug for the video camera.

The second-grade girls present a strikingly different image. (See figure 3.2.) At the beginning of the session, Ellen is sitting at the edge of her seat. Later she moves back into the seat, but then Jane moves to the edge of hers. Thus the space between them remains small. Finally, and for much of the session, they are both at the edges of their seats, sitting very close to each other, almost nose to nose compared to the boys. In all the positions in which they sit,

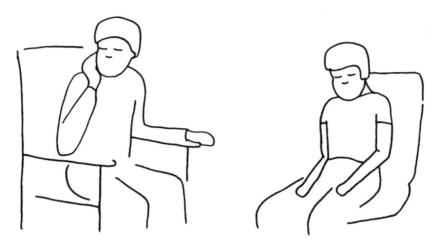

Figure 3.1. *Second-grade boys*

Figure 3.2. *Second-grade girls*

they look straight into each other's faces. When they are thinking of something to say, their eyes and heads veer away, but their bodies remain facing each other throughout.

The contrast in physical composure and level of physica' ity is in keeping with prior research on very young boys a

Amy Sheldon (personal communication, September 1988) reports that her study of the videotaped interaction of 3- to 5-year-old boys and girls in same-sex triads at play yields similar findings. (See Sheldon [1990] for other results of this study.) The boys moved around more than the girls did while playing in the same area. This difference was brought home by the video technician in Sheldon's study, who had trouble keeping the entire boys' triad in the camera's sights; no such problem arose with the girls.

Grade six. The diffuse physical alignment of the sixth-grade boys is not as marked as that of the second-grade boys, but it follows the same pattern. (See figure 3.3.) The sixth-grade boys stay in their seats, but one boy, Walt, squirms continually. The lack of direct eye contact is reinforced by Walt's frequently rubbing his eyes and playing with his fingers in his lap, his gaze firmly fixed on his fingers. Tom is less visibly restless, but he spreads his legs out in front of him and occasionally briefly drapes his right arm behind the chair. He sits aligned with the upholstered chair and therefore at an angle to Walt.

Of the sixth-grade girls, Shannon sits quite still throughout the session, with her arms on the arms of her wooden chair. At the beginning she sits at the edge of her chair, and later she sits back in

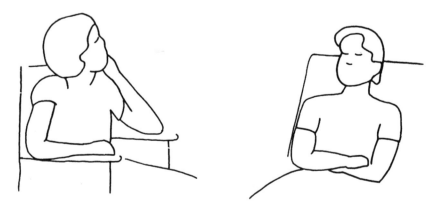

Figure 3.3. *Sixth-grade boys*

it, but she always has her body aligned to face Julia, and, although her gaze drifts away, it always returns before long to Julia. Julia sits diagonally across her armless upholstered chair in order to face Shannon head-on. Whereas the sixth-grade boy who sits in this chair spreads out across the chair, Julia draws her body up onto it. She places her left ankle on her right knee; she holds her foot and plays with her shoelaces. Although this partly occupies her gaze, she frequently returns the gaze to Shannon, in contrast with the boy at the same age level whose eyes are anchored on his hands for long periods of time. The sixth-grade girls change their physical positions a few times during the 20-minute session: Julia sits back in her chair and eventually moves forward again. Having put her left leg down, she again raises and holds it at the end. But these shifts are neither abrupt nor frequent, and the girls are always tightly aligned with each other in gaze and body posture. (See figure 3.4.)

Grade ten. In contrast to the second-grade boys, the tenth-grade boys are relatively still; they significantly change their positions only once. But the postures they maintain are marked. They begin by sitting so that their bodies are aligned with the chairs they sit in,

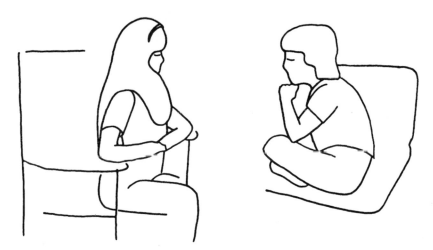

Figure 3.4. *Sixth-grade girls*

which are at an angle to each other, so their bodies are at angles to each other. In order to face each other, they would have to turn their heads; they rarely do so. For the most part, they look away and out; Todd, on the right in the upholstered chair, steals occasional fleeting glances at Richard, but Richard, on the left in the wooden armed chair, almost never looks at Todd, as if he has been forbidden, as Orpheus was forbidden to look back at his wife. Throughout the 20-minute conversation, Richard sits with his legs extended before him, and he is slouching, almost reclining, in the chair. For the first 5 minutes, Todd sits upright in his chair. But when the investigator leaves following his 5-minute visit, having just told the boys to talk about something intimate, Todd swivels around—*away* from Richard. He briefly places his hands, one on top of the other, on the back of the upholstered chair and rests his head on his hands, assuming a forlorn and weary posture. Immediately after, he leans back in the chair, extends his legs, and uses his feet to pull a wooden swivel chair on wheels into place as a footrest. As the conversation proceeds, Todd manipulates the swivel chair with his feet, alternately resting them on it and using them to push it around or away. But regardless of what he is doing with his feet, he maintains a reclining position, his back slid way down. Thus the two boys conduct their conversation with their bodies reclining, parallel to each other, their gazes fastened straight ahead. One person, seeing a brief clip of the two boys aligned in this way, commented that they look like two people riding in a car: side by side, each looking ahead, rarely looking at each other.

The tenth-grade girls provide a startling contrast. Like the sixth-grade girls, they sit across rather than aligned with the chairs in order to face each other. Whereas the boys at this age extend their legs, the girls both draw their feet up onto the chairs. Nancy, on the left in the wooden chair, sits fairly still, hardly changing her position. For a brief time, Sally, on the right, leans back, placing one arm on the back of the upholstered chair; at one point she takes a bottle of skin cream out of her purse and rubs cream on her elbows; but throughout, she sits firmly in the chair and looks steadily at her friend, who looks steadily at her.

Twenty-five-year-olds. The 25-year-old men, like the tenth-grade boys, align themselves with their chairs rather than with each other, so they end up sitting at angles to each other. Furthermore, Winston's chair, on the left, is situated slightly forward, so he has to turn his head not only to the side but also slightly back in order to face Timothy. This he does occasionally—not as rarely as the tenth-grade boys look at each other, but not often. When he listens, he looks at Timothy more often than when he speaks, but never for extended time. Timothy keeps his gaze more or less steadily ahead, which means he rarely looks at Winston. He, however, is not looking as far off in another direction as are the tenth graders.

Finally, the 25-year-old women conform to the pattern. Marsha, on the left, sits across her chair so that she is facing Pam directly, with her profile to the camera, a profile which does not perceptibly change during the 20-minute conversation. At the start she has her left leg drawn up onto her chair, and her right leg bent slightly with her right foot resting on the front edge of Pam's chair. This brings her body almost or actually in contact with Pam's. Later she extends her left leg and brings it to rest on the rest on the rear left edge of Pam's chair. Throughout, she looks directly at Pam. Thus, although Marsha stretches one leg out for a time, her legs become a physical connection to the other woman rather than being pointed out and away, like the limb extensions of the boys. Furthermore, her body remains upright, not slouched down and spread out. Pam has the wooden chair with arms; she sits squarely in it, with her arms on the arm rests, facing Marsha. Both women maintain steady and rarely broken eye contact throughout their conversation.

Discussion: are males disengaged? The impression made by viewing the physical alignment of the boys and girls and women and men in comparison to each other is that the girls and women are more closely oriented to each other. They seem more involved, one might say more conversationally coherent. When I described the pattern I was observing to a practicing therapist, she commented, "Oh, yeah. When I see families in therapy, the man never looks at his wife and never looks at me. The men are always disengaged." She remarked that the family therapy literature includes descriptions of this phenomenon. But is the lack of physical and visual alignment evidence of lack of engagement?

If gender differences are seen in a cross-cultural framework, the evaluation of lack of eye contact and physical alignment as disengagement is taking the women's pattern of showing conversational engagement as the norm. However, the anthropological literature is rich with examples of cultures in which interactants are expected not to look at each other in particular settings and interactions. For example, in many cultures, respect is shown by casting the eyes down and never looking a superior in the face. No one would conclude, however, that this means the interactants are not "engaged." Rather, in those situations, avoiding eye contact is the appropriate display of conversational involvement. The consistency of the pattern observed in these videotapes—by which the boys and men do not directly align themselves with each other physically and do not look each other in the eyes—suggests that there is a norm among them not to do so. A. L. Becker, commenting on my observation, suggested that, for men, head-on posture and gaze connote combativeness, so breaking that alignment signals and establishes friendly engagement.[4]

The conversation of the tenth-grade boys provides dramatic evidence that physical alignment away from rather than toward each other does not mean lack of engagement. As described above, the tenth-grade boys sit parallel to each other, stretched out in postures that could be interpreted as lackadaisical and careless, in one case occasionally and in the other case almost never glancing at the other. Viewing the videotape with the sound turned off could easily give the impression that these boys are disengaged. But turning the sound up reveals the most "intimate" talk heard in any of the tapes I observed.

In accordance with the procedure followed in the experiment, the investigator entered the room after the boys had been talking for 5 minutes and said, "Hi, I said I'd come back in 5 minutes? And ask you to talk in a serious or intimate way?" After he leaves, the boys snicker and chuckle briefly. Then the following interchange ensues:[5]

Todd: What the hell we supposed to talk about?
I mean I know what's bugging me.

Richard: What's bugging you?

Todd: [snicker] That we don't talk.

Richard: Who don't talk?

. . .

Todd: We're doing it again.

Richard: What?

Todd: Not talking.

Richard: I know. Well, go.

Todd: We're not even making small talk any more.
[laugh]

Richard: Right, okay. (3.4)
I mean you know.
What can I say? (3.6)
I mean,
if you meant everything you said last weekend,
and I meant everything I said. (1.0)

Todd: Well of course I did.
But I mean I don't know.
I guess we're growing up.
I mean- I don't know.
I guess I live in the past or something.
I really enjoyed those times
when we used to stay up all night long
and just you know
spend the nights over someone else's house
just to talk all night.

Richard: mhm

Todd: They were kinda fun.

Richard: Yeah that <u>was</u> fun.
(2.2)

Todd: But now we're lucky if we say anything
to each other in the hall.

Richard: Oh, all right! [challenging intonation]

Todd: I'm serious.
I remember walking in the hall
and I'd say "Hi" to you
and you'd say "Hi there"
or sometimes you'll push me in the locker,
if I'm lucky.
[laugh]
(1.4)

Richard: We ta:lk. [protesting]

Todd: Not the same way anymore.
(4.8)

Richard: I never <u>knew</u> you wanted to <u>talk</u>.

The conversation continues in this vein until the investigator enters and ends it. Todd reveals deep feelings of hurt and disappointment that his friendship with Richard is not as close as it once was.

SUMMARY: PHYSICAL ALIGNMENT

In summary, then, my analysis of the postural and visual alignment of the pairs of friends indicates that girls and boys and men and women achieve and display their involvement with each other and with the conversation in different ways. The girls and women are more physically still, more collected into the space they inhabit, and more directly aligned with each other through physical proximity, occasional touching, body posture, and anchoring of eye gaze. The boys and men do not touch each other except in playful aggression, do not anchor their gaze on each other's faces, and spread out rather than gather themselves into the space they inhabit. The boys in the youngest pairs are more physically restless, more diffused in the room both in their movements and in their gaze. The boys and men in the two older pairs are more physically still but still less directly aligned with each other in posture and gaze. However, this does not mean that the men and boys are not engaged, not involved. It simply means that their means of establishing conversational engagement are different. These differences, however, are likely to lead to negative evaluation and the impression of lack of engagement if measured by women's interactional norms.[6]

TOPICAL COHESION

The pattern of topical cohesion is analogous to that of physical and visual alignment: The girls' and women's talk is more tightly focused, the boys' and mens' more diffuse. At all ages, the girls and women exhibit minimal or no difficulty finding something to talk about, and they talk about a small number of topics. At all ages, with the exception of the tenth-grade boys discussed above, the boys and men exhibit great difficulty finding something to talk about. The two youngest pairs elaborate no topic, so they produce small amounts of talk about each of a great number of topics. The two older pairs talk about a small number of topics, but they discuss the topics on a more abstract level. At all four ages, there are differences between the genders in terms of what topics they discuss and what concerns emerge in their choice of topics. The males frequently use the room as a topical resource; the females rarely do. There are occasional references to violence in the boys' talk, never in the girls'. Finally, there is much concern among the girls with separation and avoidance of anger and disagreement. I demonstrate these findings by discussing each of the pairs in turn.

Second-grade boys. Among both the second- and the sixth-grade boys, no topic is elaborated. The second-grade boys exhibit extreme discomfort in the situation of sitting in a room with nothing to do but talk. They talk about finding something to do. They tease, tell jokes, plan future activities. They talk about what is in the room, using what Erickson (1982) calls "local resources" for topics. They look for a game to play (*Jimmy:* "What games do we- does he have.") and try to devise one (*Kevin:* "Let's play patty cake."). They do not sustain any topic for more than a few turns. They sing, make motor sounds by trilling their lips, utter nonsense syllables, utter scatological words (*Jimmy:* "You have tu tu in your panties," "and then made a fart- Here he comes!"). There are only two extended turns in the 20-minute conversation: one in which Jimmy explains a video game, and another in which he explains how to play patty cake (even though it was Kevin who proposed playing it.)

Like most of the participants in this study, the second-grade boys begin by talking about the problem at hand: Kevin asks, "What are we going to talk about?" Jimmy responds with a command, "Look at this," and makes a face by pulling his cheeks down and his mouth out. Jimmy teases Kevin:[7]

> Your hair is standing up.
> Look.
> It's still sticking up.
> Still. Still. Still. Still. Still.
> Let go.
> It's sticking up.
> No. Go like this and-
> Now it's almost down but a little-
> and then go like this.
> Go like this.
> Go like this.

Throughout this teasing, Jimmy is laughing and smoothing his own hair in demonstration. He returns to the same tease later:

> Your hair's sticking up.
> Still is.
> Your hair always sticks up.

The videotape shows no evidence that Kevin's hair was standing up, though Kevin seems to take the tease seriously, judging from his actions (he mirrors Jimmy's gesture and repeatedly smooths his hair) and words ("I didn't comb it. That's why.").

Kevin's response to the teasing is to make a gesture of shooting Jimmy. (The boys at sixth grade also make a shooting gesture; no girls do.) At other times, Kevin ignores the teasing, for example when Jimmy tells him, "I know Jerome doesn't like you at all."

The boys talk repeatedly about finding something to do:

> Kevin: You want to come over to my house one day?
> Ride my bike?

> Jimmy: What we doin' now?

> Jimmy: Look. You know what the game-
> What the game is over there-
> We play- we had that in first grade.

> Jimmy: What games do we- does he have. ["he" refers to
> the investigator]

> Kevin: I don't know.

> Jimmy: Probably only that.
> That's a dumb game isn't it.

> Kevin: Looks pretty good though.

> Jimmy: I can't wait until we play games.

> Jimmy: Well if you have something to do, do it.
> Kevin: Here he comes back in.
> What would you like to do.

> Jimmy: Play football.

> Jimmy: Would you find something to do.
> Kevin: Patty cake.
> Jimmy: [laugh] Look.
> Patty cake.
> Come on, let's do patty cake.
> Come on.

In order to generate talk, Jimmy takes the role of interviewer. He repeatedly asks Kevin, "How you doing in school?" until Kevin objects, "You don't have to keep telling me that." Jimmy also asks Kevin, "How are you playing soccer?" He then recapitulates the topics he deems appropriate to talk about:

Jimmy: I've got four things to say.

Kevin: Yeah.

Jimmy: I've got four things to say.

Kevin: Tell me.

Jimmy: You doing good in your school work, huh.

Kevin: Yeah.

Jimmy: um Play soccer good?

Kevin: Uh huh.

Jimmy: You're nice.
What was the last one?
How are you.

Kevin: Fine.

Jimmy: It's your turn.

It seems that Jimmy's model for sitting and talking is an interview, perhaps that of a child by a parent or other adult. This suggests that simply sitting and talking is not something that seems natural to do with a friend. Furthermore, at this young age, Jimmy has articulated the model that seems to characterize the conversations of all the boys and men in the tapes I viewed. "How are you?" is a routine opener, and "You're nice" a vague topic. The other two topics Jimmy names, school and sports, are indeed those that the boys and men in the study most often begin with and discuss.[8]

Second-grade girls. In topical cohesion as in physical alignment, the girls at grade two provide an astonishing contrast to the boys at the same grade level. Whereas the second-grade boys jumped from topic to topic, never fixing on one or elaborating any, and talked about activities, the second-grade girls immediately agreed on a topic that was also an activity: They told each other stories.

When the tape begins, Ellen is telling about a shared experience at a party they had both attended. Jane responds with a story about a recent incident at home when she was reading to her brother. Ellen responds with a story about having read to *her* brother. Jane's next turn is a story about another shared experience, at a restaurant. At this point the first 5 minutes are up, and the experimenter enters and says,

> Oh well folks
> remember I said I'd come back after a little bit?
> Yes so you could think of something serious
> to talk about.
> Well it's about time
> so why don't you go ahead
> and think about it
> and kind of talk about it a little bit
> and I'm gonna go away
> and come back in a little while again
> okay?

The girls follow these instructions to the letter. They huddle and whisper, apparently talking about what to talk about. They come up with a topic that is indisputably serious: For the rest of the time, they exchange stories about illness, accidents, hospitalizations, falls, and scrapes. They tell their stories in a stylized intonation pattern beginning with drawn-out rising intonation, such as Michaels and Cook-Gumperz (1979) describe for narratives told during "sharing time" in a kindergarten classroom. A particularly brief but nonetheless representative story exchange goes like this:

> Ellen: Remember
> what when I told you about my uncle?
> He went up the ladder after my grandpa?
> And he fell and um cracked his head open?

He's and you know what?
It still hasn't healed.

Jane: One time,
my uncle,
he was uh he has like this bull ranch?
In Millworth?
And the bull's horns
went right through his head.

Ellen: That's serious.

Although the girls do not explicitly tie their stories to the previous story, it is easy to track the cohesion from one story to the next. For example, in the above excerpt, not only is Jane's story similar to Ellen's in being about an accident, but it is also about an uncle and a head wound. Ellen's evaluation, "That's serious," is touching, not only because it is oriented to the investigator's instructions to talk about "something serious," but also because it is approving, in striking contrast to the mock-hostile teasing of the boys at the same age. The girls also orient their stories to each other by frequently beginning with "Remember?", reminding each other of previous shared experiences and conversations. Thus the girls could be said to discuss a single topic, serious misfortunes, with many subtopics. Moreover, they settle upon the activity of exchanging stories with no visible discomfort; rather, they seem comfortable engaging in the activity of talk.

Sixth-grade boys. In their 20-minute conversation, the sixth-grade boys touched on 55 topics. They began by mentioning school and homework and went on to such topics as cable TV, sports, sex and violence on TV, noticings about the room, other boys at school, Walt's shoes (which he takes out of a bag and hands to Tom for inspection), a rock group they play in, inflation, Nancy Reagan buying a dress for $3,000, girls, guns, videos, and their friendship. No topic extended over more than a few turns, and only two turns extended for more than a few utterances. One of these two extended turns was not exactly a turn at talk: Tom sang a song he had recently composed for their rock group. The other extended turn was a brief story about a bicycle accident (Erickson [1990] discusses bike accident stories as a conversational genre in which boys and men participate). Most turns were only a single phrase or a sentence or two in length.

Following is a representative segment of the sixth-grade boys' conversation:

Tom: Dang. This is quite a picture. [*referring to picture in room*]

Walt: uh-huh

Tom: I hate it sometimes when you're watching TV and it's really boring.

Walt: Yeah.

Tom: Yeah the only thing you ever see on TV anymore is sex and all that.

Walt: And like the crime rate's not like it really is in the real world.

Tom: I know, I mean you go to- you don't go into a department store every day and get shot.

Walt: I know.

Tom: I was watching James Bond today. They're- I don't think they're gonna have motor bikes like that. The crooks come after one detective with machine guns in their motor bike. That's what I want, a motor bike, but my dad don't like motor bikes.

Walt: Neither does mine. He says they're too dangerous.

Tom: You heard of that new song, it's called Miss Dance? Flash Dance?

Walt: Yeah.

Tom: I don't know, she's on a dance team or something.

Walt: I like that song.

Tom: Wha- what /??/ report card this time, Oh Jesus.

Walt: Pretty good. They went up.

As this segment shows, the boys switch topics often, and no topic is extensively elaborated; references are elliptical and brief. The boys do, nonetheless, negotiate a lot of agreement—a style that has been associated with girls (see Eckert 1990).

This is not to imply that the sixth-grade boys never discuss interpersonal relationships. Following is a segment in which they do.

Tom: Man school is getting a pain.

Walt: I know.

Tom: Everyone's starting
to get on each other's back.
Mrs. Gladdis-

Walt: I hope Jerry don't come anymore.
I don't know why.

Tom: I used to like him- but now-
I don't know what happened
but he lost my interest.

Walt: Sid's been suspended man.

Tom: I know.
Man I- I'll flunk if-
I just went down a little bit in school.
Because Sid give-
What's that guy's name?
Jerry? Jimmy? That likes Sid.
Sitting right by me talking.

Walt: I know.

Tom: While I can't even sing and he sings right.
I don't want to sing.

Walt: Yeah I know what you mean.

Tom: I sing the new songs we write.
Man, we got to fix up our rock group
or we're going to be out of it man.

I chose this segment about other children at school and their relationships because it is closest to the girls' in topic. But it also shows
that the topics are not elaborated: The references are elliptical and
brief. On a more surface level, it is noticeable that many of Tom's
topic-introducing turns (11 in all) begin with "man" as a discourse
marker.

Sixth-grade girls. As with the second graders, the sixth-grade
girls present a staggering contrast with the boys of the same age.

Both the girls and the boys at this age begin by talking about
what happened at home the night before. But they focus on very
different aspects of their home interaction. Of the sixth-grade boys,
Tom opens the topic by mentioning objects: a jet plane and a
television.

> Tom: Man-
> Yesterday?
> We were sitting and watching cable?
> Some big old jet came flying by
> sounded like he was going to land.
>
> Walt: [laughs]
>
> Tom: And then our cable went out yesterday.
>
> Walt: Ours too.

In contrast, when the sixth-grade girl who opens the talk tells about
what happened at home the night before, she recounts an emo-
tionally charged incident involving a family member:

> Julia: Um: Guess what happened last night.
>
> Shannon: What.
>
> Julia: Um ... I went um, okay
> Last night, um- my brother um, my b-
> Okay my dad said,
> "Julia you gotta pick up, by yourself."
> And /?/ I said,

> "Well, if my brother doesn't have to"
> and so me and my dad
> got into a big fight and everything yknow?
> And u:m, oh go:d.
> And I bit him.
> I couldn't <u>believe</u> it.
> Oh go:d!

Shannon: Oh my go:sh. Did he get mad?

Julia: Yeah, but not- not right now just-
      I went in my room.
      I locked the [door.

Shannon: [Uhuh.

Julia: Oh go:d.

Not only is Julia's turn about a family member. It is longer than any turn produced by the boys at the same age; indeed it is a story. And it is about a particular kind of family interaction: a fight. Most of the sixth-grade girls' talk concerns intimacy and fights: the concern that fights destroy intimacy. Whereas "man" is the characteristic discourse marker of one of the sixth-grade boys, the discourse marker that peppers Julia's talk at topic boundaries or points of unease is "go:d" or "oh go:d," of which there are 20 occurrences. Moreover, the crux of Julia's story is expressed in dialogue: her father's demand that she pick up after herself ("'Julia you gotta pick up, by yourself'") and her protest that her father was asking more of her than of her brother ("'Well, if my brother doesn't have to'").

Immediately after this, Julia raises the topic that accounts for most of the talk in this conversation: her friendship with another girl, Lizzie, which ended because of Lizzie's flareups of anger:

> Julia: I'm so glad that Lizzie, um,
>   and the rest're not mad at me anymore.

After a short spate of talk on this topic, Shannon raises a different one: "Tomorrow I want to go ice skating." Both girls then evaluate their own ice skating ability negatively, after which Julia declares that she hopes she and Shannon will remain friends in high school, even though they will be going to different high schools. The danger of their falling out is raised by reference, again, to Lizzie: " 'Cause you know that's what happened to you and Lizzie." Shannon protests that "Lizzie did that herself." In the midst of a short exchange of remarks on relationships at school and on an upcoming picnic, Julia gives Shannon a friendship pin. Before long, however, they are back with Lizzie:

> Shannon: Too bad you and Lizzie
> are not good friends any more.
>
> Julia: I know.
> Go:d, it's- she's so <u>mean</u> sometimes.
>
> . . .
>
> And then- what was so sad
> she just- gets <u>ma:d</u> at you
> all of a sudden.
> And like if she does somethin'
> I don't like,
> I mean, I just- I don't <u>li:ke</u> it,
> I mean, I don't get ma:d at her!

Their discussion continues at length about how Julia wanted and tried to be friends with Lizzie, but Lizzie made the friendship impossible. Here, as elsewhere, much of Julia's concern centers around the destructive effects of anger and her claim that people should not get mad at each other (for example, "My mom does things that I don't like a lot, an- I just- I mean I don't get <u>ma:d</u> at her.") Another related concern Julia expresses is the pain of losing friendships ("It <u>hurts</u> when you lose your best friend.")

The next three topics are raised, rather suddenly, by Julia. On the surface, they seem like topic switches, but on a deeper level, they are new phases of the same topic: concern with separation and loss. After more talk about Lizzie, Julia leaps forward in her chair and says,

Julia: Oh! I forgot
I have to ask you something.
Have you ever felt that you're adopted?

The girls go on to discuss who is or might be adopted and why they think so. Then Julia says, "I like getting a friend and keeping it fore:ver," thereby initiating a discussion of friendship which leads to a discussion of children's relationships with peers and parents, including criticism of children who are too self-centered and demanding or too catered to by their parents. Not surprisingly, one girl who comes in for such criticism is Lizzie. All these topics are concerned with intimacy and fear of its loss. Finally, Julia says, without apparent cohesion with previous talk,

When um, well-
I hate for my parents to be divorced.
That's what happens when they get in fights.
I think that they're just gonna say,
"Well, I'm gonna get a divorce."
And then whenever,
whenever they get in fights,
just rushed through my mind Lizzie and Jonah.

The coherence, however, is clear: Julia suspects that Lizzie's unacceptable character is the result of her parents' divorce; she believes that expression of anger leads to separation, so when her parents fight, she's afraid they will get divorced and her character will be ruined like Lizzie's ("I'd hate to be turned into a snob.").

Before leaving discussion of the sixth-grade girls' conversation, I will remark on two related aspects of their speaking style, which are very noticeable when one hears their voices. First, their talk has a highly stylized sing-song quality that is easily recognizable as typical of teenage girls' talk. This quality results from sharp shifts in pitch, strong emphatic stress on many words, intonation which rises and remains steady at the end of phrases, and elongation of vowels.

Second, much of their talk is made up of what I term "constructed dialogue" (Tannen 1989), as seen above when Julia performs her fear that her parents are "just gonna say, 'Well, I'm gonna get a divorce.'"

Tenth-grade girls. There is such a striking resemblance between the tenth-grade and sixth-grade girls that I will discuss the tenth-grade girls here and contrast the tenth-grade boys after.

The tenth-grade girls spend the first 5 minutes giggling, joking, and laughing. Their 20-minute talk includes 18 topics, but 16 of these are found in the first 5 minutes, before they settle down to talk. After the investigator's reminder at the 5-minute mark that they should talk about something "serious and/or intimate?" the girls quickly fix upon two related topics: Nancy's problematic relationships with her boyfriend and her mother. There is a parallel to the situation with the sixth-grade girls in that the talk focuses on one of the girls' problematic relations with other people, and in that these topics are raised by the other girl:

> Sally: Talk about John.
> That's serious and/or intimate.

Although John does eventually become the topic of talk, that does not happen immediately. After a few noncommittal exchanges (such as Nancy's "What about him?"), Sally suggests the second of Nancy's problems:

> Nancy: Okay.
> Well, what do you want to talk about?
> Sally: Your mama, did you talk to your mama?

It emerges that Nancy and Sally were part of a group on a trip to Florida, from which Nancy summarily left at her mother's insistence. The rest of the talk elaborates this experience, focusing on Nancy's departure and the effect of her trip and her early return on her relationships with John and other male friends.

There are other ways that the talk of the tenth-grade girls is similar to that of the sixth-grade girls. Although not quite as stylized as those of the younger pair, the intonation patterns here too tend toward sing-song intonation, elongation of vowels, marked shifts in pitch, and constructed dialogue. There are also words and expressions that Nancy uses which are reminiscent of Julia, such as "go:d" and "I couldn't believe [it]". This pattern emerges immediately after they settle on a topic. Sally tells Nancy about the effect of Nancy's departure on her friends:

Nancy: Go::d, it was ba::d.
        I couldn't believe she made me go home.⌉
 Sally: ⌊I thought
        it was kind of weird though,
        I mean, one minute we were going out
        and the next minute Nancy's going
        "Excuse me, gotta be going." [both laugh]
        I didn't know what was goin' <u>on,</u>
        and Mary comes up to me
        and she whispers,
        (the whole place knows),
        "Do you know that Nancy's going home?"
        And I go, "What?" [both laugh]
        "Nancy's goin' home."
        I go "Why::?"
        She goes, "Her mom's makin' her."
        I go, [makes a face], "ahh."
        She comes back and goes, "Nancy's left."
        Well I said, <u>Well</u> that was a fine thing <u>to do,</u>
        she didn't even come and say goodbye."
        And she starts boiling all over me,
        I go [mimicking yelling] "<u>All ri::ght!!</u>"
        She was upset, Marge,
        I was like "Go::d"⌉
Nancy: ⌊I just had to go home.
        [clears throat] I know, when I was going home,

> I said, I said, "Mom, could we hurry up?
> I want to go home and call John."
> I'm going, I was trying to tell her,
> "Look, I gotta do something
> or I'm going to go nu::ts!"

Sally: Did she say anything?

Nancy: Not really.

As in a teenage girl's narrative I have described elsewhere (Tannen 1988), the dialogue is central, and the most frequent verb introducing the dialogue is a form of the verb "go" ("I go 'Why::?'"). An alternate and also frequent form for introducing dialogue (Tannen 1986b) is "be + like" followed by not so much what someone said but what someone was feeling like, as displayed in an utterance: "I was like 'Go::d'." The intonation contours are exaggerated, and the pivotal events are relationships among people and the speaker's feelings about them.

Tenth-grade boys. Whereas the patterns that link the girls' and women's conversations are fairly constant across the ages, the tenth-grade boys' conversation is partly anomalous among the boys and men, and partly conforming to pattern. Although they do not look at each other, neither do they look aimlessly around the room, as did the second- and sixth-grade boys. Similarly, they do not use objects in the room as resources for talk. Unlike the two younger pairs, but not unlike the oldest, they talk at length on each topic.

Although it includes many intertwined subtopics, the tenth-grade boys' talk revolves around two related topics, each one reflecting the preoccupation of one of the boys. Both topics grow out of the boys' relationships, feelings, behavior, and conversations that arose during a party they attended the night before. Richard's main concern is his drinking: When he took Anne home after the party, she told him he behaves badly when he drinks and should either learn to drink moderately or stop drinking altogether. Todd's main concern is his feeling of alienation from Richard and the group. This sense of being left out, not fitting in, was triggered the night before when Richard walked out of the party to talk privately with Mary.

In the following excerpt, Richard introduces his concern by using constructed dialogue, though not the extreme intonation contours that characterize the girls' talk:

> Richard: When I took Anne home last night she told me off.
> Todd: Really?
>
> . . .
>
> Richard: You see when she found out what happened
> last Thursday night between Sam and me?
> Todd: uhuh
> Richard: She knew about that.
> And she and she just said
> and then she started talking about drinking.
> You know?
> And after I thought,
> "Well, look at the hypocrite
> look at the hypocrite who's talking,"
> and I s- I didn't say that.
> And then she said, you know,
> "You, how you hurt everybody when you do it.
> You're always cranky."
> And she just said, "I don't like it.
> You hurt Sam.
> You hurt Todd.
> You hurt Mary.
> You hurt Liz."
> And I said,
> "Oh, make Richie out to be the alcoholic."

Richard calls Anne hypocritical because, later in the same conversation, "she goes, 'can't wait to go to Joe's tomorrow night and get drunk off our behinds'." But he takes her criticism seriously and repeatedly returns to the question of whether he should try to limit his drinking or stop it altogether.

Todd repeatedly returns to the topic of his feelings of alienation. The first topic of talk is an upcoming dance which Richard raised in reference to his talk with Mary the night before: Richard is concerned because Mary does not have a date for the dance. Rather than sharing Richard's sympathy for Mary, Todd responds with a comment that reveals that he doesn't have a date for the dance either ("See, I don't feel like asking anyone"). Furthermore, he says he went on a date with a girl named Janet, but it just made him feel bad because "It gets boring after one date. [laugh] That's all there is to it." Later on, as Richard continues to talk about his conversation with Anne, Todd again brings up his own concern: He has felt cut off from Richard, and he resents the time Richard spends with Mary.

Richard: I mean, when she told me, ...
yknow I guess I was kind of stunned. (5.6)
I didn't really drink that much.

Todd: Are you still talking to Mary,
a lot, I mean?

Richard: Am I still talking to Mary?

Todd: Yah, 'cause that's why-
that's why I was mad Friday.

Richard: Why?

Todd: Because.

Richard: 'Cause why?

Todd: 'Cause I didn't know why you all just wa-
I mean I just went back upstairs
then y'all never came back.
I was going "Fine. I don't care."
I said, "He's going to start this again."

Rather than pursuing Todd's complaint about his disappearing from the party with Mary, Richard returns to the topic he raised at the outset: his concern that Mary has no date for the upcoming dance ("God, I'm going to feel so bad for her if she stays home."). After a brief response in which he expresses no sympathy for Mary ("She's not going to stay home, it's ridiculous. Why doesn't she just ask somebody?"), Todd returns to his own concern, his sense of alienation: "I felt funny again last night" because "I felt so out of place." Todd goes on to explain that that was why he himself disappeared:

> Todd: And, ah, I just felt out of place again,
> so I just ran out on the back courts
> for a second
> and I came back
> and there's this big search party looking for me.

For the tenth-grade boys, as for the girls of the same age, friendship alliances are of central concern, and one way these are observed is in party behavior: who is there and who defects.[9]

The boys, like the girls, talk about other people. They also spend a lot of time putting others down. But whereas the girls are specific in criticizing the behavior of others (the way they dress, that Lizzie gets angry), the boys (especially Todd) put them down in a general way (Mary and Richard's mother have "zero brains," someone else is "such a clod").

The pattern of topical cohesion mirrors the pattern of physical alignment displayed by the tenth-grade boys. Just as Richard and Todd sit parallel to rather than facing each other, so their conversation proceeds on parallel tracks. As has been shown, Richard and Todd simultaneously discuss two main topics, one of concern to each of them, whereas the girls at grades six and ten focus on the troubles of one of them. Furthermore, as has also been shown, each boy frequently brings up his own topic in immediate response to the other's expression of his. Moreover, both boys frequently downplay or dismiss the concerns expressed by the other. Several examples of this have already been given: For example, it was seen earlier that Todd denied that Mary deserves sympathy for having no date for the dance. Other examples follow.

In the next example, when Todd explains why he doesn't want to ask Janet to the dance, Richard expresses lack of understanding:

Todd: I felt so bad when she came over
and started talking to me last night.

Richard: Why?

Todd: I don't know.
I felt uncomfortable, I guess.

Richard: I'll never understand that. [laugh]

Richard responds to Todd's repeated expressions of feeling left out by reassuring him that he shouldn't feel that way. For example, in response to Todd's remark that he felt out of place at the party the night before, Richard argues that Todd's feelings are unfounded:

Richard: How could you feel out of place?
You knew Lois, and you knew Sam.

Todd: I don't know.
I just felt really out of place
and then last night again at the party /?/
I mean, Sam was just running around,
he knew everyone from the sorority.
There was about five.

Richard: Oh no he didn't.

Todd: He knew a lot of people.
He was- I don't know.

Richard: Just Lois,
he didn't know everybody.

. . .

Todd: Hum. I felt /?/
I just felt really out of place that day,
all over the place.
I used to feel, I mean

Richard: Why?

Todd: I don't know.
I don't even feel right in school anymore.

Richard: I /?/ don't know, last night, I mean-

Todd: I think I know what Ed Rierdon and them
feels like now. [laugh]

Richard: [laugh] No I don't think you feel as bad
as Ed Rierdon feels.

Todd: I'm kidding.

Richard: Uh- uh. Why should you?
You know more people-

Todd: I can't talk to anyone anymore.

Richard: You know more people than me.

Richard responds to Todd's expression of feeling out of place by
first asking why he feels that way and then countering Todd's
answers by arguing that the reasons are unjustified: Todd knows a
lot of people; Sam and he know no more; Todd couldn't feel as bad
as he says.

Todd responds to Richard's concern with his drinking in a similar way, by denying that it is a problem:

Richard: Hey, man, I just don't feel-
I mean, after what Anne said last night,
I just don't feel like doing that.

Todd: I don't think it was that way.
You yourself knew it was no big problem.
[moves chair and puts feet up]

Richard: Oh, Anne-
Sam told Anne that I fell down the levee.

Todd: It's a lie. [hissing]

Richard: I didn't fall.
I slipped, slid.
I caught myself.

Todd: Don't worry about it.

Richard: But I do kinda.
I feel funny in front of Sam.
I don't want to do it in front of you.

Todd: It doesn't matter
     'cause sometimes you're funny
     when you're off your butt.

This pattern supports Eckert's (1990) observation that high school boys do talk about personal topics, but they do so differently from girls. In this study, though they all talk about personal problems and concerns, the tenth-grade boys nonetheless differ from the sixth- and tenth-grade girls. Whereas both pairs of girls focus on the problems of one, elaborating and agreeing in their perspectives on it, each boy talks about his own concerns and disagrees with the concerns expressed by the other in order to downplay his problems. The closest congruence in point of view displayed by the boys is when they join in ridiculing someone else; for example, they laugh at Richard's mother for having "zero brains" because, noticing that something was bothering Todd, she thought he might be displeased "because we put the cake out so early."

Women frequently express dissatisfaction with the way that men respond to their concerns. Whereas they would like the men to express understanding and sympathy, what they hear is downplaying of the problem (or, if the problem is acknowledged, advice about how to solve it). Observation of the tenth-grade boys supports the suggestion that such dissatisfaction is the result of cross-cultural differences. Neither boy shows dissatisfaction with the other's response. Denying the basis for the other's complaint seems not to be a failure of empathy (as women might perceive it) but rather a means of reassurance.

Twenty-five-year-old men. The men in the oldest pair exhibit palpable difficulty finding a topic, marked not by giggling, chuckling, or joking, but by displays of cerebral effort and strain. They begin with school:

Timothy: You know looking back
     seriously speaking uh
     I'm sorry I didn't major in psych.

This topic lasts only a short time, after which Winston articulates their discomfort at finding a topic:

> Winston: Ain't exactly easy
> just to come up with something
> along these guidelines.
>
> Timothy: Boy it sure isn't.
> (25.0)

This conversation is slow, both in interturn and within-turn pacing and pausing. However, the 25-second pause shown in this example is a particularly long one, evidence of the difficulty the men experience finding a topic for talk that seems "serious." Soon, however, they agree upon the topic that occupies them for the rest of the time:

> Winston: How about marriage.
>
> Timothy: That's a serious enough topic.
>
> Winston: Serious topic,
> and it doesn't receive a lot of attention.
>
> Timothy: Dave told me he thinks
> it will be easier to get to heaven ...
> as a married person.

The men take seriously their charge to find a serious topic, and they seem to believe "serious" requires a topic of general as well as personal significance, something about which one can make a meaningful contribution ("it doesn't receive a lot of attention").

Although marriage is a topic of personal concern to everyone, these men's conversation about marriage is carried on for the most part on a theoretical level:

> Timothy: Why do you think uh
> so many marriages ain't makin' it?
> That's uh you know a broad question.
>
> Winston: I think most people rush into it
> for one thing. (6.0)
> Just can't wait to get married.

Timothy: I think uh I think people
   a lot of people
   and I'm not saying I <u>do</u>
   but a lot of people
   don't have an adequate or uh mature you know
   definition in their lives of what love is.
   You know uh I don't know
   'cause a lot of the strife
   you know in my opinion
   in marriages and relationships
   is because the person has the uh
   you know selfish attitude.

Elsewhere, the men agree that women are more concerned with getting married than are men. Winston explains that he learned in an adolescent psychology course that "women have their whole personality on their ability to relate with the opposite sex yknow whereas men just, it's them and the world more yknow."

Late in the discussion the men turn to their personal positions on the topic, but even these are kept fairly abstract. Timothy is dating a woman, and he says he is considering marrying her, but he explains that he feels very cautious, because a commitment to marriage will be forever.

 and uh yknow I'll admit for the first time
 I'm thinking about it seriously
 but uh that's just what it says
 thinking about it seriously though
 I'm no closer to making any kind of a commitment
 than I was before.

After a few more remarks about how he and his girlfriend are maintaining a "wait-and-see attitude" until she finishes school, Timothy shifts the focus to Winston by saying, "Yknow I don't just want to talk about my situation." After a pause, Winston responds:

Well mine's with school
and school is just the epitome
of being an unsettled person.

Winston seems to be implying that, being a student, he is feeling too unsettled to think about marrying. But he expresses this feeling indirectly, as a general statement about school.

Similarly, earlier in the conversation, Winston says that sometimes men become shy of relationships because they have been hurt:

I think a lot of people start off
like maybe when they're young
they might have the attitude
of what they think is 100 percent give
and then they get torched.
Or what they think is torched.
And it's liable to just yknow give them yknow
a pretty shy attitude towards it
for a long time.

This statement suggests that Winston may have been hurt, or "torched," in a romantic relationship, but if this is so he does not say it. He does not say anything about any relationships of his own.

The men's talk is characterized by slow pacing (there is no overlapping), formal register ("strife," "receive" instead of "get"), and numerous hesitations, fillers, and formulaic expressions ("seriously speaking," "you know in my opinion," "let's face it"). They make broad and relatively abstract rather than personal statements which they hedge by stressing that these are only their opinions.

Twenty-five-year-old women. The conversation between the last pair, women in the oldest age group, covers their own relationship with each other as well as their personal life plans and choices. The conversation has an odd tension about it, which I believe results from an early misunderstanding. After briefly mentioning a few topics like school, leisure activities, and general inquiries ("How have you been?"), Pam turns the talk to their friendship:

> Pam: Yeah one thing about you
> is that you always agree with me.
> One thing I like.
> Marsha: That's because we pretty much think alike.
> Pam: Yeah but you agree with-
> I mean, you know how to talk to people
> when they have a problem.
> One of your favorite expressions is,
> "I hear ya- I hear that."
> Marsha: Oh, god.
> Pam: That's the way you say it.
> Marsha: I'll have to remember that.

Pan seems to intend her observation that Marsha knows "how to talk to people" as praise, but Marsha seems to interpret it as a put-down, perhaps implying, "You are wishy-washy; you have no mind of your own." Marsha appears embarrassed by Pam's mimicry of her voice ("One of your favorite expressions is 'I hear ya- I hear that.'"), as if the mimicry were mockery.

This tension drives the ensuing conversation. Marsha explains that, because others in her family talk a lot, she "kind of learned to sit back and listen." But she explains that appearing to agree can mask not listening:

> Marsha: But sometimes what people don't realize
> is that I'm not really like um hm,
> that I don't, yknow-
> it's a bad habit,
> kinda tune 'em out.
> Pam: Well you know how not to argue
> because you know how to be patient
> and listen to what they have to say.
> (1.6)
> Marsha: Well (1.9)
> Pam: You always done that with me.

> I don't think you've ever argued with me,
> though.
>
> Marsha: Sure we have.
> That's what we're doing right now.

Marsha refers to the characteristic which Pam identified, showing verbal agreement, as "a bad habit," claiming that rather than showing good listenership, it often masks not listening ("tune 'em out"). Pam's attempts to assure Marsha that "that's good" never really take hold.

As seen in the preceding as well as the following excerpts, Pam begins to sound like the sixth-grade girl, Julia, insisting that friends do not fight, whereas Marsha, as if to proclaim her independence of thought, maintains that they do disagree:

> Marsha: um god Pam, I know we've had arguments before
>
> . . .
>
> Marsha: We disagree on a lot of things, though.
> um school for instance.
> And since you've got such a positive
> ⌈um yeah well no you've got such-
> Pam: ⌊Positive? You saw me a few minutes ago.
> [Investigator briefly interrupts]
> Marsha: You've got such a positive attitude.
> Pam: No I don't.
>
> . . .
>
> Marsha: See that's one thing that we do disagree on.
> Maybe I'm not a very confident person,
> I guess, and you've got my share.⌉
> Pam: ⌊Well- I- well.
> what do you think of my computer science attitude
> right now.

Pam's insistence that Marsha is more positive and has more confidence sounds like accusation and criticism rather than praise. Just as

Pam resisted the description of herself as agreeable, Marsha resists the description of herself as positive and confident.

The conversation includes many small struggles such as these. For example, Marsha seizes upon Pam's remark that she hopes to get an A in a course as evidence of their differences:

Marsha: See, that's another thing.
You're always, I mean
I'm just so bad about this.
I get into a class
and the highest that I really hope to get
is may- a B,
if I can get, a B, out of a course,
I guess it's just been so long
since I have gotten an A.

Pam: That you don't think about it?

Marsha: Yeah well I don't think that it's attainable.

Pam: I don't either.

Marsha: But Pam, every, yknow, every semester
when we start school,
it's like you talk about it though,
that you've got to get an A in this course.

Pam: A's, I get B's.
I try but I never get A's,
I always get B's.
Well, maybe except in my psychology courses,
maybe.
But not all of 'em.

As with Marsha's suggestion that Pam is confident, Pam seems to take Marsha's suggestion that she gets good grades as an accusation to be resisted rather than as a compliment to be accepted. As if in counterattack, Pam points out that Marsha did well in a religion class ("You do well on the tests, 15 out of 15" whereas "I hadn't even read those chapters"). Symmetrically, Marsha disclaims merit ("It's a lot of common sense").

Much of the remaining conversation focuses on the women's plans for the future. Marsha tells Pam she is an excellent tutor and should consider becoming a teacher; Pam encourages Marsha to take up tutoring too and argues against Marsha's disclaimer that she doesn't have enough patience. Throughout their conversation, the women seem to be vying for the distinction of having little confidence, low grades, lack of ability, and poor communication skills; when they do admit to positive qualities, they belittle them. They seem to be engaged in a ritual which Beeman (1986), describing Iranian interaction, terms "getting the lower hand." But whereas Beeman explains that this strategy reflects status differences in Iranian society, Pam uses self-denigration to achieve equality by claiming to be the same as Marsha.

SUMMARY: TOPICAL COHESION

Examining the eight videotapes in this study provides a view of each pair of friends as unique, with unique concerns and styles of speaking, but also of some patterns that are shared by friends of the same gender. It seemed easier for the girls and women to choose topics and talk about them, they devoted more talk to fewer topics, and their topics more often focused on personal and specific concerns. The youngest girls exchanged stories about misfortunes. The sixth- and tenth-grade girls engaged in "troubles talk" focused on the troubles of one of the girls. The 25-year-old women discussed their comparative personalities and plans for the future. Of major concern to them, as to the sixth-grade girls, was interpersonal disagreement and harmony.

The boys and men divided into two groups. The boys at the second- and sixth-grades devoted small amounts of talk to each of a great number of topics. The youngest boys, moreover, repeatedly expressed the desire to find something to do. The tenth-grade boys and 25-year-old men, despite signs of discomfort, did talk at length about a limited number of topics. The men discussed a potentially personal topic, marriage, in relatively impersonal and abstract terms. The tenth-grade boys discussed topics of intense personal concern, but they differed from the girls who discussed personal concerns in a number of ways: First, each tended to focus on and return to his own concerns and downplay the concerns expressed by the other. Second, one confronted the other directly with a complaint about their relationship, in contrast to the girls who complained about relationships with others who were not present.

CONCLUSION: THE CONGRUENCE OF POSTURE AND TOPIC

Although I have discussed physical alignment and topical cohesion separately, the patterns observed in these two elements of conversational involvement are analogous and operate simultaneously in conversation. In both the alignment of posture and gaze and the development of topics, the girls and women focused more tightly and more directly on each other than did the boys and men. For example, the tenth-grade boys' parallel focus on their own concerns in contrast to the sixth- and tenth-grade girls' joint focus on the concerns of one, is a verbal analogue to the way they were sitting: The tenth-grade boys sat aligned but parallel, both looking out rather than at each other, whereas the girls sat facing and looking at each other.

I have cautioned, however, against concluding with value judgments such as that girls and women are more "engaged" than boys and men. For example, although the girls are more visibly aligned with each other both physically and topically, nonetheless, in keeping with patterns observed by researchers such as Goodwin (1990) and Eder and Sanford (1986), the girls express complaints against friends who are not present, whereas the complaint of the boy who expresses a significant complaint is aimed directly at his friend who is present.[10] In this sense, the tenth-grade boys could be said to be more "engaged" with each other than any of the girls in these tapes. Moreover, the talk of the tenth-grade boys displayed more intense intimacy than that of any of the other pairs, although their physical postures were indirectly rather than directly aligned, and they never looked directly at each other.

This and other observations of the boys and men demonstrate that, although they did not align themselves directly to each other, they were clearly orienting to each other and conversationally involved. This is a crucial point. One of the main observations of Gumperz's (1982) analysis of cross-cultural communication is that ways of signalling intentions and meanings, ways of constituting the context of communication, are not universal but culturally relative. I suggest, following Gumperz and Maltz and Borker (1982), that gender differences can be understood as cultural differences. It is likely that one source of the most frequent complaint by women about their relationships with men—that men do not listen to them—issues from differences demonstrated by this study: Perhaps the men do not face them head on and maintain eye contact, do not pursue a topic at as great a length as women do, and respond to concerns either by raising a topic of their own concern or by denying or belittling the basis for the woman's concern. If cross-cultural differences are at play, then these patterns of conversational involvement do not indicate lack of listenership but rather different norms for establishing and displaying conversational involvement.

That the girls and women showed less discomfort finding a topic, elaborated topics at greater length, physically squirmed less, and generally looked more physically relaxed, seems to indicate that they found it easier to fulfill the assigned task of sitting in a room and talking to each other than did the boys and men. This may be because, as Lever (1978) and Goodwin (1990) observe in natural interaction, sitting inside and talking is a familiar and frequently self-selected activity for girls, whereas boys more frequently choose to play games outside, in groups. If this is true, then the experimental task was a more familiar one to the girls and women than to the boys and men.

Support for this view is found in a description by Hoyle (1993) of boys' play at home. Hoyle observed that her son frequently played in their basement with one or another friend, providing,

Hoyle believed, counterevidence to the claim that boys do not play in pairs. But the activity she observed her son and his friends engaging in is sportscasting: While playing indoor basketball or video games, the boys spontaneously took the role of sports announcer, casting themselves as players and providing a running account of their actions in sports announcer register. This self-selected activity supports the prior research, also supported by the present study, in a number of dramatic ways. First, the boys elected to play a game rather than talk. Second, finding themselves in a pair, they used sportscasting to bring more characters into the room. Finally, by taking the role of sports announcer, they distanced themselves from the immediate intimacy of one-on-one interaction. Hoyle notes that her son and his friends did not engage in sportscasting when there were more than two boys present.

My discussion has made use of what Geertz (1983) calls a "cases and interpretations" approach to analysis, as distinguished from a "rules and instances" approach. Analysis of a single pair of friends at each of four age levels is limited in scope but allows analysis in depth. Examining what was said and how each individual's behavior is oriented to the behavior of the other provides insight into the process of conversational involvement that would not be available using other methods alone.

My analysis supports the growing body of research suggesting that there are gender-related patterns in conversational interaction but also that there are similarities and overlaps woven into the web of differences. Taking a cross-cultural view of gender differences in establishing and displaying conversational coherence allows us to see similarities and differences that explain negative impressions made by cross-gender conversations without casting blame or making negative value judgments.

NOTES

This chapter was originally published in *Conversational Organization and Its Developments,* edited by Bruce Dorval (Norwood, NJ: Ablex Publishing Corp., 1990,

167–206). I am grateful to Bruce Dorval for the enlightening opportunity to study these videotapes and to A. L. Becker for helpful comments and discussion on a pre-final draft. I also benefitted from discussion with panelists Penelope Brown, Penelope Eckert, Marjorie Harness Goodwin, and Amy Sheldon, when I presented findings from this study as part of a panel entitled "Gender Differences in Conversational Interaction" at the 1988 Georgetown University Round Table on Languages and Linguistics, Georgetown University, Washington DC, March, 1988. Papers presented in that panel, including a slightly revised and significantly shortened version of this one, appear in *Discourse Processes,* 13(1), 1990, and, with the exception of this one, are reprinted in *Gender and Conversational Interaction,* edited by me and published by Oxford University Press (1993). This is the longer study that provided material for chapter 9 ("'Look at Me When I'm Talking to You!': Cross Talk Across the Ages") in *You Just Don't Understand: Women and Men in Conversation.* Indeed, as I explain in the introduction to that book, this study was crucial in motivating me to further study gender and language and to write that book. The current chapter includes much more detail than the chapter in *You Just Don't Understand,* and it includes the conversation of young adults which I omitted from the book. My thanks to Greta Patten for drawing the illustrations.

1. I refer to the oldest pairs of speakers as "25-year-olds" in order to avoid the cumbersome but more accurate label, "24- to 27-year-olds." The fifth age level in the study, involving speakers of approximately 20 years of age, was eliminated because it was not possible to identify female and male pairs for which legible transcripts were available and which did not include speakers of radically different cultural backgrounds.

2. Research design always represents a trade-off. Ethnographically oriented researchers would never elicit discourse in an experimental situation and would argue, with justification, that the discourse thus elicited is not "natural." However, as Wolfson (1976) argues, all "natural" speech is simply speech natural to the situation in which it is produced. The experiment designed by Dorval elicits speech natural to the odd situation in which it was produced. Moreover, it provides the otherwise impossible opportunity to compare how speakers of different ages and genders speak in this odd, but comparable, situation.

3. Scheflen (1976, p. 55) describes what I am calling "tight" or "direct" alignment as a "closed mutual orientation" and "full face-to-face orientation." He does not, however, address gender differences. Aries (1982, p. 127) notes that "men have been reported to assume more relaxed, open postures than women," a finding supported by her own study. These studies do not, however, address the issue of mutual orientation. Citing Exline (1963) as the pioneering source, Henley (1977, p. 160) observes, "Probably the most accepted finding in this area is that women engage in more eye contact than do men, especially with each other."

Frances (1979) corroborates this and also finds that male subjects in her study "made significantly more seat position shifts and leg position shifts during the experimental sessions than did female subjects" (p. 531). Thus previous research on posture and gaze has identified the patterns that I observed in the videotapes of friends talking but has not examined these patterns in terms of coherent gender-related strategies for establishing conversational involvement.

4. When he sat down to join me in the conversation in which he made this observation, Becker began by moving his chair. Having found it positioned directly facing mine, he moved it slightly to the side and swiveled it slightly, so that, when he sat in it, he was sitting at an angle to me rather than facing me head-on. This he did without thought, automatically, although we both recognized the result in a flash of recognition and amusement.

Becker also pointed out that the world of animals provides numerous instances of the behavior of individuals which seems, at first glance, unrelated but turns out, upon close observation, to show finely tuned coordination. An example he offered is two geese seemingly self-absorbed in preening their feathers with movements that precisely mirror each other, as if they were performing the same dance to the same music.

Animal behavior also provides a parallel to Becker's suggestion that head-on posture and gaze may suggest combativeness: Horse and dog trainers warn that looking these animals directly in the eye will ready them for attack. The association of gaze with aggressiveness, and the analogy of primate behavior, are also noted by Henley (1977).

5. Transcription is based on that provided by Dorval. I have, however, checked and refined transcription of passages I cite, and have laid them out in "chunks" or "lines" which I believe are easier to read because they reflect the natural prosodic and rhythmic chunking of spoken discourse. Three spaced dots (. . .) between lines of transcript indicate a small number of lines has been omitted; three unspaced dots (...) indicate a brief untimed pause. Numbers in parentheses show measured pause length in seconds; spaces between lines of transcript indicate segments taken from different sections of the transcript. In a number of the transcripts, the word *god* appears. I have chosen to render it with a small *g* because I believe it is a formulaic usage, not intended to refer to a deity but used automatically as a discourse marker. (See Schiffrin 1987 for discussion of discourse markers.) In instances where the word *god* begins a sentence, I render it with a capital as I would the first word of any sentence. Colon (:) indicates elongation of preceding vowel sound. <u>Underline</u> indicates emphatic stress. /?/ indicates unintelligible word(s). Brackets show overlapping speech; ⌐ indicates latching (no interturn pause); - indicates a glottal stop (abrupt cutting off of sound); punctuation indicates intonation, not grammatical convention.

6. The suggestion, made earlier, that psychotherapeutic norms of interactive behavior may reflect women's norms is supported by a psychiatric study (reported in *Psychiatry '86,* August 1986, pp. 1,6) which found that women are more effective therapists when they are new to the field, but that the gender difference in effectiveness fades among experienced psychotherapists. This suggests that psychotherapeutic training and experience teach men to behave in ways that women do with minimal or no training or experience.

7. There are many aspects of the way the boys and girls and women and men in these videotapes talk that suggest gender-related differences other than those discussed in this chapter. For example, as supported by this excerpt, it seems likely that agonistic teasing is more frequently done by boys than girls. Furthermore, Jimmy's use of imperatives is in line with Goodwin's (1990) and Sachs's (1987) findings that boys use more imperatives than girls at play, and Gleason's (1987) observation that fathers use more imperatives than mothers when talking to their children. The pattern of interaction I found among these boys is very similar to that described by Leaper (1988) for five-year-old boys in his study.

8. It is difficult to resist observing that Jimmy seems to be taking a leadership role in this interaction. He has the only extended turns; he gives orders and instructions; he teases and initiates most of the conversational moves. Of the sixth-grade boys, Tom seems to be a leader, since he raises most of the topics and is the main speaker, with Walt contributing and supporting. Of the 55 topics covered in their interaction, Tom raises 40. Walt raises 15 topics, of which 6 were noticings about the room (for example, "That's a funny-looking picture"). The interaction between the sixth-grade girls sheds light on the complexity of the question of leadership. One might initially be inclined to identify Julia as the leader. Of 14 topics discussed, Julia raises 12. Furthermore, most of the discussion centers around Julia's relationship with Lizzie, her concerns about keeping friends, and her anxiety about separation and loss. When the experimenter briefly enters the room at the 5-minute mark, it is Julia who talks to him. Yet it is Shannon who "chooses" the topic of Julia's relationship with Lizzie as the one to fulfill the experimenter's request. Similarly, most of the tenth-grade girls' talk is about Nancy, but it is Sally who proposes Nancy's problems as a topic for talk. Thus the issue of leadership is suggested by many of the excerpts presented here, but it is a complex one that requires much further analysis.

9. Another common theme is the intimacy exhibited in spending the night at each other's houses. This emerges in the conversations of the sixth-grade girls as well as the tenth-grade boys. It is also the issue which causes a dispute among middle-school girls analyzed by Eder (1990).

10. Goodwin (1990) finds that boys tend to express disagreement directly, whereas girls tend to do so indirectly, to other girls. This is not to say, however,

that girls never express conflict directly to each other. Eder (1990) and Goodwin and Goodwin (1987) discuss situations in which they do.

REFERENCES

Aries, Elizabeth. 1982. Verbal and nonverbal behavior in single-sex and mixed-sex groups: Are traditional sex roles changing? Psychological Reports 51.127–34.

Becker, A. L. 1988. Language in particular: A lecture. Linguistics in context: Connecting observation and understanding. Lectures from the 1985 LSA/TESOL Institute, ed. by Deborah Tannen, 17–35. Norwood, NJ: Ablex.

Beeman, William O. 1986. Language, status, and power in Iran. Bloomington: Indiana University Press.

Eckert, Penelope. 1990. Cooperative competition in adolescent "girl talk." Discourse Processes 13:1. Reprinted in Gender and conversational interaction, ed. by Deborah Tannen, 32–61. Oxford and New York: Oxford University Press, 1993.

Eder, Donna. 1990. Serious and playful disputes: Variation in conflict talk among female adolescents. Conflict talk, ed. by Allen Grimshaw, 67–84. Cambridge: Cambridge University Press.

Eder, Donna, and Stephanie Sanford. 1986. The development and maintenance of interactional norms among early adolescents. Sociological studies of child development, vol. 1, ed. by Patricia A. Adler and Peter Adler, 283–300. Greenwich, CT: JAI Press.

Erickson, Frederick. 1982. Money tree, lasagna bush, salt and pepper: Social construction of topical cohesion in a conversation among Italian-Americans. Analyzing discourse: Text and talk. Georgetown University Round Table on Languages and Linguistics 1981, ed. by Deborah Tannen, 43–70. Washington, DC: Georgetown University Press.

Erickson, Frederick. 1990. The social construction of discourse coherence in a family dinner table conversation. Conversational organization and its development, ed. by Bruce Dorval, 207–38. Norwood, NJ: Ablex.

Exline, Ralph V. 1963. Explorations in the process of person perception: Visual interaction in relation to competition, sex, and need for affiliation. Journal of Personality 31.1–20.

Frances, Susan J. 1979. Sex differences in nonverbal behavior. Sex Roles 5:4.519–35.

Geertz, Clifford. 1983. Local knowledge: Further essays in interpretive anthropology. New York: Basic Books.

Gleason, Jean Berko. 1987. Sex differences in parent-child interaction. Language, gender, and sex in comparative perspective, ed. by Susan U. Philips, Susan Steele, and Christine Tanz, 189–99. Cambridge: Cambridge University Press.

Goodwin, Marjorie Harness. 1990. He-said-she-said: Talk as social organization among black children. Bloomington: Indiana University Press.

Goodwin. Marjorie Harness, and Charles Goodwin. 1987. Children's arguing. Language, gender, and sex in comparative perspective, ed. by Susan U. Philips, Susan Steele, and Christine Tanz, 200–248. Cambridge: Cambridge University Press.

Gumperz, John J. 1982. Discourse strategies. Cambridge: Cambridge Universisty Press.

Henley, Nancy M. 1977. Body politics: Power, sex, and nonverbal communication. New York: Simon and Schuster.

Hopper, Paul. 1988. Emergent grammar and the a priori grammar postulate. Linguistics in context: Connecting observation and understanding, ed. by Deborah Tannen, 117–34. Norwood, NJ: Ablex.

Hoyle, Susan M. 1993. Participation frameworks in sportscasting play: Imaginary and literal footings. Framing in discourse, ed. by Deborah Tannen, 114–44. New York and Oxford: Oxford University Press.

Leaper, Campbell. 1991. Influence and involvement: Age, gender, and partner effects. Child Development 62:797–811.

Lever, Janet. 1978. Sex differences in the complexity of children's play and games. American Sociological Review 43:471–83.

Maltz, Daniel N., and Ruth A. Borker. 1982. A cultural approach to male–female miscommunication. Language and social identity, ed. by John J. Gumperz, 196–216. Cambridge: Cambridge University Press.

Michaels, Sarah, and Jenny Cook-Gumperz. 1979. A study of sharing time with first grade students: Discourse narratives in the classroom. Proceedings of the Fifth Annual Meeting of the Berkeley Linguistics Society, 647–60.

Sachs, Jacqueline. 1987. Preschool boys' and girls' language use in pretend play. Language, gender, and sex in comparative perspective, ed. by Susan U. Philips, Susan Steele, and Christine Tanz, 178–88. Cambridge: Cambridge University Press.

Scheflen, Albert E., with Norman Ashcraft. 1976. Human territories: How we behave in space-time. Englewood Cliffs, NJ: Prentice-Hall.

Schiffrin, Deborah. 1987. Discourse markers. Cambridge: Cambridge University Press.

Schiffrin, Deborah. 1988. Sociolinguistic approaches to discourse: Topic and reference in narrative. Linguistic change and contact, ed. by Kathleen Ferrara, Becky Brown, Keith Walters, and John Baugh, 1–17. Austin, TX: University of Texas Press.

Sheldon, Amy. 1990. Pickle fights: Gendered talk in preschool disputes. Discourse Processes 13:1.5–31. Reprinted in Gender and conversational interaction, ed. by Deborah Tannen, 83–109. New York and Oxford: Oxford University Press, 1993.

Tannen, Deborah (ed.) 1984. Coherence in spoken and written discourse. Norwood, NJ: Ablex.

Tannen, Deborah. 1986a. That's not what I meant!: How conversational style makes or breaks your relations with others. New York: William Morrow. Paperback: Ballantine.

Tannen, Deborah. 1986b. Introducing constructed dialogue in Greek and American conversational and literary narrative. Direct and indirect speech, ed. by Florian Coulmas, 311–32. Berlin: Mouton.

Tannen, Deborah. 1987. Repetition in conversation: Toward a poetics of talk. Language 63:3.574–605.

Tannen, Deborah. 1988. Hearing voices in conversation, fiction, and mixed genres. Linguistics in context: Connecting observation and understanding, ed. by Deborah Tannen, 89–113. Norwood, NJ: Ablex.

Tannen, Deborah. 1989. Talking voices: Repetition, dialogue, and imagery in conversational discourse. Cambridge: Cambridge University Press.

Tannen, Deborah. 1990. You just don't understand: Women and men in conversation. New York: William Morrow. Paperback: Ballantine.

Wolfson, Nessa. 1976. Speech events and natural speech: Some implications for sociolinguistic methodology. Language in Society 5.189–209.

CHAPTER FOUR

Conversational Strategy and Metastrategy in a Pragmatic Theory

The Example of *Scenes from a Marriage*

This chapter was written with Robin Tolmach Lakoff, who was my professor at the University of California, Berkeley, at the time. We were not thinking of this work as contributing to the language and gender literature; rather, we intended it to be a contribution to the literature on pragmatic theory. We were interested in how the communicative styles of two speakers could be seen to interact with each other on a number of levels. The theoretical introduction and conclusion were written by Lakoff and represent her individual work; I wrote the sections that analyzed examples from the Bergman play. Together, we had viewed the film on television and discussed the screenplay. It was only in retrospect that I observed that the styles exhibited by the characters Marianne and Johan, wife and husband in the play, could be seen to typify female and male styles of interaction.

In the introduction to the chapter, Lakoff addresses the issue of the use of fictional dialogue for linguistic analysis, a relatively unusual practice for contemporary linguists. She then briefly summarizes her own theoretical system for understanding communicative styles as reflective of four points on a continuum: distance, deference, camaraderie, and clarity. These are the styles in terms of which the linguistic strategies used by Marianne and Johan can be understood. Our subsequent analysis shows that Marianne's style combines deference and camaraderie, whereas Johan's displays distance. Marianne "frequently talks (and acts) like a child. She habitually puts herself down, and she puts up a smokescreen of nonstop verbiage made up of impressionistic romanticism or a flurry of questions." Johan, in contrast, "uses sarcasm and irony, pontification, generalization and abstraction, and high-flown language in complex sentences." When one partner uses strategies typical of the other, s/he is summarily corrected.

In our analysis, we show that these two speakers alternately use different linguistic devices to achieve similar ends, similar devices to achieve different ends, and the same devices toward the same ends. Lakoff shows that these three alternatives replicate the basic semantic relations of synonymy, homonymy, and identity; hence she suggests the terms "pragmatic synonymy," "pragmatic homonymy," and "pragmatic identity" to characterize these interactional processes. In the chapter's final section of analysis, we examine the use of questions in a single scene in order to show how the couple's verbal strategies operate on these three levels. This chapter, then, offers a detailed example of how linguistic analysis of an extended segment of discourse can shed light on how stereotypically female and male styles can operate in interaction with each other.

INTRODUCTION:
A THEORY OF COMMUNICATION COMPETENCE

THE QUESTION OF ARTISTIC VERISIMILITUDE—the relationship between the representation and the reality—is one of the more intriguing issues in a theory of aesthetics. Until now, linguists have largely been isolated from this area of philosophical speculation because it seemed irrelevant to our interests and impervious to our methodology. But as we get more involved in the formal analysis of naturalistic conversations—through tape recordings or transcripts—we are struck, often, in a perverse way by their apparent unnaturalness, their difficulty in being understood. Compared, say, with the dialog in a play or a novel, naturalistic conversation strikes us as not what we expected, not working by preconceived pattern.

We would not claim that constructed dialog represents a reality lacking in transcripts, but rather that artificial dialog may represent an internalized model or schema for the production of conversation—a competence model that speakers have access to. If, then, we are interested in discovering the ideal model of conversational strategy, there is much to be gained by looking at artificial conversation first, to see what these general, unconsciously-adhered-to assumptions are; and later returning to natural conversation to see how they may actually be exemplified in literal use. Thus, we are not claiming that the artificially-constructed dialog we are going to discuss literally represents natural conversation, but rather that one can inspect a different level of psychological reality and validity through the use of literary data, and in this paper we will illustrate how such work might responsibly be done. In this sense, our work here is in support of a theory of communicative *competence*—the knowledge a speaker has at his/her disposal to determine what s/he can expect to hear in a discourse, and what s/he is reasonably expected to contribute, in terms of the implicitly internalized assumptions made in her/his speech community about such matters.

We need, then, some notion of what parameters the speaker can use as reference points in determining how a contribution can appropriately be made in a particular context. The speaker must know first what sort of extralinguistic facts pertain: what kind of a conversation it is, how well the participants know one another, what sorts of things must be communicated; and additionally, what mode of communication is the normal style for each speaker—what can be expected of each from prior acquaintance and/or a priori assumptions based on age, sex, social position, and so on. All this specific information need not be directly represented as part of the speaker's specifically linguistic competence; but what is reflected in her/his pragmatic grammar is a general schema, a theory of communicative competence.

It has been suggested (Lakoff 1979) that there are four principal foci of communicative competence: that is, that while competence itself comprises a continuum, with infinite possible points prescribing the appropriate interaction for an individual in a particular setting, these infinite possibilities are organized in terms of four targets, and which target is relevant depends on the participant's perception of her/his role in the conversational setting as s/he perceives it. For each person, in any culture, there is a more or less unconscious sense of an idealized interactional human being: an idealized human being behaves in *such* a way, in *this* setting. The four points as they have been specified are: (1) Distance; the aim is to inspire separateness and privacy. The least intrusiveness is the best. Hostility is not expressed, therefore, by confrontation (which is unthinkable) but by sarcasm, irony, impersonality. (2) Deference; the aim is to avoid imposition. That is, unlike distance, deference allows interaction as long as the speaker does not attempt to get the upper hand. Hostility cannot be directly expressed, but can be made clear enough through questions or silence, for instance. (3) Camaraderie; the aim here is to acknowledge interrelationship. Participants are to express their equality and their feelings toward one another, friendly or hostile. The ideal is to be totally open, though openness in this mode is as politeness is to the others—it can be conventional, though this is not perceptible to people who do not use this mode as an ideal. (4) Clarity; where the other modes implicitly or explicitly expressed relatedness, or the fact that the relationship was an important part of the communication, clarity is used where the pure expression of factual information is at issue. Hence closeness or distance is not an issue. This is not normally a possibility in ordinary dyadic communication; it is found with television newscasters (sometimes), or with certain forms of lecturing.

Our task, then, is to select a constructed example of dialog; discover what each participant's preferred strategy is, or whether what it appears to be is what it really is, and why; and talk about how the writer's realization of his/her characters' styles represents a reality that has correlates, if not necessarily direct ones, in more naturalistic texts.

THE SELECTION OF *SCENES FROM A MARRIAGE*

We could have selected any of a wide variety of examples. We had to choose between plays, movies, novels, television—just as a start. We felt that a genre that used dialog as the principal expository means of expressing characters and their relationships would make our position clearest. Novelists have many other techniques to fall back on, but for a playwright, dialog and its concomitant extralinguistic behavior is all the audience has to go on. Interpretation must be done by the viewer, or listener—as in actual conversation; whereas in the novel, the novelist by careful selection and description can do a lot of his/her own interpretive work.

We wanted to find a contemporary example, as that would be the clearest to us. We needed something with a lot of dialog between relatively few people—so that register differences would be minimized, and we would be dealing with something like a minimal pair. We would want to examine as many interactional types between as few participants as possible—to see what a single individual's or two people's strategies were, when confronted by different contexts. That is, we wanted the largest possible sample of conversational situations involving the smallest number of people to maximize the contributions and types of contributions of each.[1]

We wanted something that was supposed to approximate natural conversation, and that would seem to its audience to be natural and something they could identify with, something similar to their intuitive assumptions about ordinary conversation. Ideally, we would have preferred a contemporary American setting. But when practical factors were considered—amount of text, availability, and so on—what we found to be the most useful compromise was the screenplay of the original six-hour television version of Ingmar Bergman's *Scenes from a Marriage*. There is the possibility that Swedish couples do not talk to each other as American couples do, but the successful reception of this work in the United States, both in the shortened movie version and the complete version presented several times on PBS in 1979, indicates that we can understand perfectly well what's going on, and that although there may be slight differences in a particular choice of how to say a particular thing, the general concepts are universal, or at least the same in Swedish and American conversation.[2]

SURFACE HARMONY AND UNDERLYING DISCORD: THE FRAMEWORK OF *SCENES FROM A MARRIAGE*

Scenes from a Marriage consists of six scenes (i.e., six acts), tracing the relationship of a couple, Johan (a research psychologist) and Marianne (a lawyer). Scene One, entitled "Innocence and Panic," introduces Johan and Marianne as "the perfect couple" (they are even interviewed for a magazine article). In this scene there is only a hint of difficulty, in that Marianne is pregnant and has an abortion. Scene Two, "The Art of Sweeping Under the Rug," contains stronger hints that both are dissatisfied, but all is under the surface. In Scene Three, "Paula," Johan announces that he has a lover and leaves Marianne. Scene Four, "The Vale of Tears," shows Johan visiting Marianne at their house some time after the separation. In the Fifth Scene, "The Illiterates," they meet at his office after hours to sign their divorce papers, and end up in a brutal battle. Scene Six, "In the Middle of the Night in a Dark House Somewhere in the World," shows Marianne and Johan meeting secretly; they are both married to new spouses and have been having an affair with each other for a year.

When Johan and Marianne are presented in the early sections of *Scenes from a Marriage,* their cooperative metastrategy is to avoid recognition of their deep differences and dissatisfactions—while maintaining the illusion of open communication and rapport. This can be seen clearly in Scene One, when Johan and Marianne have just witnessed a grisly display of mutual viciousness by their friends Peter and Katarina. After the friends leave, Marianne tells Johan that Peter's and Katarina's problem is "They don't speak the same language," and she contrasts this with what she sees as the happy situation between Johan and herself:

> (1) Marianne: Think of us. We talk everything over and we understand each other instantly. We speak the same language. That's why we have such a good relationship. [p. 26][3]

Evidence to the contrary abounds in this very discussion. Johan does not agree with Marianne at all; he contends that Peter's and Katarina's problems stem from money, and he responds to Marianne's analysis with characteristic sarcasm: "You and your languages" [27]. Marianne, in turn, chides him, "You always confuse the issue" [27].

In Scene Four, after they have separated, Marianne admits that she never understood Johan at all. In that scene, she responds to something Johan said:

> (2) Marianne: I don't know what you're talking about. It seems so theoretical. I don't know why. Perhaps because I never talk about such big matters. I think I move on another plane. [119]

After Johan's reply, she continues:

(3)　Marianne:　I remember you always talked and talked. I used to like it, though I hardly ever took any notice of what you said when you held forth at your worst. [120]

In the last scene, they both acknowledge this lack of communication:

(4)　　　Johan:　It just struck me that you and I have begun telling each other the truth.

Marianne:　Didn't we before? No, we didn't. . . . [196]

. . .

Johan:　Did we even know that we kept things secret?

Marianne:　Of course we lied. I did, anyway. [197]

This recognition of their lack of communication comes belatedly and painfully. While they are together, Marianne steadfastly insists that she and Johan "speak the same language," despite evidence to the contrary.

The tension between the appearance of successful communication and the underlying unacknowledged discord is the theme of Scene Two, entitled "The Art of Sweeping Under the Rug." When one partner tries to express dissatisfaction, the other "sweeps it under the rug" to maintain the appearance of harmony. In the beginning of this scene it is Marianne who expresses dissatisfaction:

(5)　Marianne:　Just think about it. Our life's mapped out into little squares—every day, every hour, every minute. And on every square it's written down what we're supposed to do. The squares are filled one by one and in good time. If there's suddenly an empty square we're dismayed and scrawl something onto it at once.

Johan:　But we have our vacation.

Marianne:　(*With a laugh*) Johan! You haven't a clue to what I mean. On our vacation we have more of a sched-

ule than ever. It's all Mummy's fault, actually.
And your mother's not much better.

Johan: (*Laughing*) What have the dear old ladies done
wrong?

Marianne: You don't understand anyway, so there's no point
talking about it. [44–45]

Later in the same scene, Marianne makes another attempt to
confront the problems in their marriage. She calls Johan and asks
him to meet her for lunch. During that meeting, she suggests that
they take a trip together in order to bring them closer together, but
Johan is unenthusiastic, and she gives up the idea. In the conversation below, she again declares that communication between them is
open, and Johan agrees with this interpretation, although we know
from the next scene that he too is deeply dissatisfied with their
relationship; in fact, he is having an intense love affair with another
woman.

(6) Marianne: (*Searchingly*) Has something happened, Johan?

Johan: Nothing. Absolutely nothing. I swear.

Marianne: We're pretty honest with each other, you and I.
Aren't we?

Johan: I think so.

Marianne: It's awful to go around bottling things up. One
must speak out, however painful it is. Don't you
think?

Johan: (*Irritably*) Hell, yes. What time is it?

Marianne: One fifteen.

Johan: My watch is always stopping. What were you
saying? Oh yes, honesty. I suppose you mean
over sex, to put it bluntly.

Marianne: Sometimes I think we ...

Johan: People can't always live cheek by jowl. It would
be too tiring.

Marianne: Yes, *that* is the big question.

Johan: Anyway, I must go now. [66–67]

In this dialog, Marianne purports to believe in talking about everything, and Johan sweeps the matter under the rug by proclaiming that some things (especially sexual) are better not talked about.

Later in the same scene, Johan and Marianne switch roles. He tries to confront their problems, and she sweeps them under the rug using devices characteristic of her style. Denying that there is anything wrong, she obstinately states that things are fine.

(7)   Johan: Must it always be that two people who live together for a long time begin to tire of each other?

Marianne: We haven't tired.

Johan: Almost.

Marianne: (*Indulgently*) We work too hard—that's what's so banal. And in the evenings we're too tired.

. . .

Marianne: But we like each other in every way.

Johan: Not in that way. Not very much anyhow.

Marianne: Oh yes, we do. [72]

In this interchange, it is Marianne who blames their personal problems on circumstance ("We work too hard").

When Johan persists in trying to articulate their difficulties, Marianne deflects the confrontation:

(8)   Johan: It's just that our life together has become full of evasions and restrictions and refusals.

Marianne: I can't help it if I don't enjoy it as much as I used to. I can't help it. There's a perfectly natural explanation. You're not to accuse me and give me a bad conscience about this.

Johan: (*Kind*) You needn't get so upset!

Marianne: (*Hurt*) I think it's all right as it is. God knows it isn't passionate, but you can't expect everything. There are those who are much worse off than we are.

Johan: Without a doubt.

Marianne: Sex isn't everything. As a matter of fact.

Johan: (*Laughing*) Why, Marianne!

Marianne: (*On the verge of tears*) If you're not satisfied with my performance you'd better get yourself a mistress who is more imaginative and sexually exciting. I do my best, I'm sure. [72–73]

In another reversal, it is now Johan who blames the problem on maternal interference, and Marianne who rejects the idea:

(9) Johan: Sometimes I wonder why we complicate this problem so frightfully. This business of lovemaking is pretty elementary, after all. It was surely never meant to be a huge problem overshadowing everything else. It's all your mother's fault, if you ask me. Though you don't like my saying so.

Marianne: I just think it's so damn superficial of you to talk like that. [73–74]

At the end of this discussion, it is Marianne who espouses the distance strategy, proclaiming that some things (particularly sexual) are better not discussed:

(10) Marianne: Let me tell you this. You can talk too much about these things.

Johan: (*Giving up*) I suspect you're right.

Marianne: I know you're supposed to tell everything and not keep anything secret, but in this particular matter I think it's wrong.

Johan: (*Who has heard this before*) Yes, you're probably right.

Marianne: (*Following up her advantage*) There are things which must be allowed to live their life in a half-light, away from prying eyes.

Johan: (*Total retreat*) You think so?

Marianne: I'm quite convinced of it. . . . [75]

This, then, is the metastrategy of Johan's and Marianne's communication with each other. They agree to maintain a surface of harmony and deny their underlying discord. Each one resists the other's attempts to confront their problems, or, put another way, each one can attempt to confront their problems in the safety of the knowledge that the other will deny them. In Scene Five, after their separation, Marianne recognizes this:

(11) Marianne: . . . Has it struck you that we never quarreled? I think we even thought it was vulgar to quarrel. No, we sat down and talked so sensibly to each other. And you, having studied more and knowing more about the mind, told me what I *really* thought. What I felt *deep down*. I never understood what you were talking about. . . . And all our subsequent discussions as to why we didn't get any pleasure out of making love. Neither of us realized that they were warnings. Red lights and stop signals were flashing all around us. But we only thought that was as it should be. We declared ourselves satisfied. [155–56]

PRAGMATIC RELATIONSHIPS

In maintaining this declaration of satisfaction, Johan and Marianne employed verbal strategies that were characteristic of their own styles and different from the other's. A close examination of the linguistic forms taken by their conversational contributions reveals that their conversation shows a pattern of relationships between deep and surface structure that replicates, on the pragmatic level, the basic semantic relations of synonymy, homonymy, and identity. That is, Marianne's and Johan's utterances alternately evidence:

I. Pragmatic synonymy or paraphrase. They use different linguistic devices to achieve similar ends.

II. Pragmatic homonymy or ambiguity. They use similar linguistic devices to achieve different ends.

III. Pragmatic identity. They use the same device toward the same ends.

INDIVIDUAL STYLES

Before proceeding to examples of pragmatic identity, synonymy, and homonymy, let us examine Johan's and Marianne's characteristic styles. Each one's style is made up of habitual use of linguistic devices according to the broad operating principles outlined above. Marianne's style reflects a combination of deference and camaraderie. She frequently talks (and acts) like a child. She habitually puts herself down, and she puts up a smokescreen of nonstop verbiage made up of impressionistic romanticism or a flurry of questions. Johan's style, on the other hand, is distancing. He uses sarcasm and irony, pontification, generalization and abstraction, and high-flown language in complex sentences. When one of the partners uses devices characteristic of the other, s/he is summarily corrected. Their differing styles create, on the surface, dissimilar-looking utterances, but in terms of the deeper intentions, they can be seen as cooperative.

Many of these devices are seen in the dialog that has already been quoted. For example, Marianne repeatedly states that things are fine, clinging to romantic unreality in a childlike way:

(1) Marianne: We speak the same language. That's why we have such a good relationship. [26]

(6) Marianne: We're pretty honest with each other, you and I. Aren't we? [66]

(7) Marianne: But we like each other in every way.
       Johan: Not in that way. Not very much anyhow.
  Marianne: Oh yes, we do. [72]

Thus, when confronted with the problems of their sexual relationship, Marianne begins by denying that there is anything wrong. When this fails, she pouts like a child and claims helplessness:

(8) Marianne: I can't help it if I don't enjoy it as much as I used to. I can't help it. There's a perfectly natural explanation. You're not to accuse me and give me a bad conscience about this. [72]

Not only does Marianne herself act like a child. At other times, she treats Johan as if he were a child. For example, when he asks for help in cutting a nail, she chides him:

(12) Marianne: . . . What do you *do* to your nails? [98]

She habitually uses a kind of teasing in place of expressing anger at Johan:

(13) Marianne: You're sillier than I thought. . . . [28]

The confrontation about their sexual relationship ends with Marianne indulging in a frenzy of this sort of teasing:

(14) Marianne: (*Kissing him*) You're kind anyway, even if you *are* an idiot.
       Johan: Then it's lucky I'm married to you.
  Marianne: (*Kissing him*) You have your great moments, but in between you're horribly mediocre.
       Johan: At our age tens of thousands of brain cells snuff out every day. And they're never replaced.
  Marianne: (*Kissing him*) With you it must be ten times as many, you're so silly. [76–77]

Along with her "playful" criticism, Marianne showers Johan with physical affection, a classic Batesonian double bind (Bateson 1972).

At the outset of Scene Three Johan returns unexpectedly to their country house where Marianne is about to go to bed alone. The ensuing conversation reveals that Marianne and Johan had a fight on the phone when they talked last, and that when she immediately called him back, he was not at home. This fact, combined with his surprising arrival late at night, gives her reason to suspect that something is wrong. After making some offhand comments about the telephone argument, Marianne launches a long and irrelevant soliloquy about life-as-it-should-be:

(15) Marianne: . . . Sometimes everything seems utterly point-less. Why should we grudge ourselves all the good things in the world? Why can't we be big and fat and good-tempered? Just think how nice it would make us. Do you remember Aunt Miriam and Uncle David? They were perfect dears and got along so well together, and they were so *fat!* And every night they lay there in the big creaky double bed, holding hands and content with each other just as they were, fat and cheerful. Couldn't you and I be like Aunt Miriam and Uncle David and go around looking comfortable and safe? Shall I take my curlers out? [83]

This passage combines Marianne's characteristic use of denial by romanticism as well as her use of nonstop verbiage. Another form of this device is seen when she produces a barrage of questions. She greets Johan with a series of offers of food combined with random references to irrelevant details. The stage directions supply a nonverbal analogue to her verbal strategy, just as in Example (14), when Marianne showers Johan with a display of physical affection.

(16)   *Before he has time to take his coat off, she flings her arms around his neck, hugs him, and gives him four loud kisses.*

> Marianne: Here already! You weren't coming until tomor-
> row. What a lovely surprise. Are you hungry?
> And me with my hair in curlers. How good of
> you to come this evening. The children are
> asleep, we went to bed early. There was nothing
> on TV and we thought it would be nice to have
> an early night. The girls and I have been dieting
> today. Would you like an omelette or a sand-
> wich and some beer?
>
> Johan: That sounds good.
>
> Marianne: Or would you like a real meal? Shall I fry some
> eggs and bacon? Or heat some soup? [81]

And yet again, in the scene in which Marianne suggests that they take a trip together, she makes so many alternative suggestions that none of them can be taken seriously:

> (17) Johan: Where did you think of going?
>
> Marianne: Anywhere. We've never been to Florence, for in-
> stance. Or what about the Black Sea? That's an
> idea. Or Africa? There are some fantastically
> cheap trips to Morocco. Or Japan. Suppose we
> went to Japan! [64]

Marianne's and Johan's contrasting styles can be seen in the very first scene in which they are interviewed for a women's maga-zine. When asked to describe themselves, Johan launches a long speech full of self-praise, but Marianne can't think of a thing to say:

> (18) Johan: Yes. It might sound conceited if I described my-
> self as extremely intelligent, successful, youthful,
> well-balanced, and sexy. A man with a world con-
> science, cultivated, well-read, popular, and a good
> mixer. Let me see what else can I think
> of ... friendly. Friendly in a nice way even to
> people who are worse off. I like sports. I'm a good

family man. A good son. I have no debts and I pay
my taxes. I respect our government whatever
it does, and I love our royal family. I've left
the state church. Is that enough or do you want
more details? I'm a splendid lover. Aren't I, Marianne?

Mrs. Palm: (*With a smile*) Perhaps we can return to the question. How about you, Marianne? What do you
have to say?

Marianne: Hmm, what can I say ... I'm married to Johan
and I have two daughters.

Mrs. Palm: Yes ...

Marianne: That's all I can think of for the moment. [4]

Thus, Johan is comfortable talking himself up—albeit ironically—
while Marianne is not. In contrast, she is comfortable putting herself
down. When the interviewer misinterprets something Marianne
says, Marianne takes the blame:

(19) Marianne: No, I didn't mean that actually. In fact, I meant
just the opposite. You see how badly I express
myself. . . . [14]

Johan's most characteristic strategy is sarcasm. This has already
been seen in a number of examples; for instance, in their early
discussion about their relationship, when Johan counters, "You and
your languages" [27], as well as the following:

(5)   Johan: What have the dear old ladies done wrong? [45]

Other examples abound. For instance, in the same discussion:

(20)   Johan: You're suffering from mother persecution mania.
[49]

In Scene Three, after Johan has announced that he is leaving Marianne in order to live with his girlfriend, Paula:

(21)   Johan: . . . I'm not taking anything with me except perhaps my books, if you have no objections. . . . [89]

In Scene Five, Marianne and Johan meet to sign their divorce papers:

(22) Marianne: . . . But I think I'm free now and can begin to live my own life. And how glad I am!

Johan: Allow me to congratulate you. [155]

In Scene Six, Marianne has answered Johan's question about her sex life with her new husband; Johan is not happy with her answer:

(23)   Johan: (*Fiercely*) Do you think I care about your orgasms with that goddamn slob and his blood pressure? You're welcome to them. I'm full of admiration for your complete emancipation. It's most impressive. You should damn well write a novel. I bet you'd be applauded by Women's Lib. [205]

In addition to sarcasm, Johan characteristically pontificates; he talks in broad generalities, using high-flown language. For example, when Marianne in Scene Three makes reference to the fact that when she called him back the night before (presumably at their home in the city) he did not answer the phone, Johan launches a pompous diatribe aimed at bureaucrats:

(24) Marianne: I called you right back, but you must have pulled the plug out.

Johan: I was pretty tired last night. I'd been out all day at the institute with the zombie from the ministry. You wonder sometimes who these idiots are who

sit on the state moneybags and determine our
weal and woe. [82]

In the scene in which Marianne attempts to express her dissatisfaction with their life, Johan uses all his habitual devices to evade
the confrontation. He blames her discontent on a physical cause,
and a peculiarly feminine one:

(25)   Johan: Is it the curse?

      Marianne: You always think it's that.

      Johan: Well, isn't it? [44]

Later, he evades a direct request for information with an ironic
rhetorical question:

(26) Marianne: Do you like coming home?

      Johan: *(Kindly)* Is everything so awfully complicated to-
          day? [48]

He is sarcastic, in a line previously cited:

(27) Marianne: If only I were sure that it's we who have chosen
          [our life], and not our mothers.

      Johan: You're suffering from mother persecution mania.
          [48–49]

He evades another direct information question with pontification:

(28) Marianne: Did you *want* your life to be like this?

      Johan: I think that life has the value you give it, neither
          more nor less. I refuse to live under the eye of
          eternity. [49]

He uses the same device later on, in Scene Five, following the
passage cited above as Example (11):

(29) Marianne: . . . We declared ourselves satisfied.

Johan: I think that these retrospective expositions are awfully boring and unnecessary. [156]

These examples show how Marianne and Johan more or less consciously use their strategies for their individual advantage. But their strategies also work together to powerful effect, a force of which they are unaware, but which, as we shall see, serves to keep them together and drive them apart at once.

To take one example, in Scene Four Johan has come to visit Marianne in their home. They have been separated for some time. Johan's relationship with Paula is deteriorating. He is lonely.

(30)   Johan: Do you know what my security looks like? I'll tell you. I think this way: loneliness is absolute. It's an illusion to imagine anything else. Be aware of it. And try to act accordingly. Don't expect anything but trouble. If something nice happens, all the better. Don't think you can ever do away with loneliness. It is absolute. You can invent fellowship on different levels, but it will still only be a fiction about religion, politics, love, art, and so on. The loneliness is nonetheless complete. . . . [118]

Johan continues in this vein for four times the length of the passage quoted. Finally Marianne comments, in a previously cited response:

(2)   Marianne: I don't know what you're talking about. It seems so theoretical. I don't know why. Perhaps because I never talk about such big matters. I think I move on another plane. [119]

Johan's response to Marianne's implicit complaint about his philosophical style is, of course, sarcasm:

(31)   Johan: (*Roughly*) A more select plane, oh. A special plane
                reserved for women with a privileged emotional
                life and a happier, more mundane adjustment to
                the mysteries of life. Paula too likes to change
                herself into a priestess of life. It's always when she
                has read a new book by some fancy preacher of
                the new women's gospel. [119–120]

This passage also shows Johan's tactic of attacking women as a
group, rather than Marianne in particular, in keeping with his habitual strategy of avoiding direct confrontation by generalizing. To use
an example cited earlier, when talking about his dissatisfaction with
their marriage, Johan expresses his dissatisfaction in general terms,
and Marianne immediately answers in terms of their particular life
together:

(7)   Johan: Must it be that two people who live together for a
                long time begin to tire of each other?
      Marianne: We haven't tired. [72]

Again, at the end of this discussion, when Marianne attacks Johan in
a teasing style, he accedes to her ploy by talking generally (and
academically), and she responds by referring to him personally once
more:

(14) Marianne: (*Kissing him*) You have your great moments, but
                in between you're horribly mediocre.
        Johan: At our age tens of thousands of brain cells snuff
                out every day. And they're never replaced.
      Marianne: (*Kissing him*) With you it must be ten times as
                many, you're so silly. [77]

Johan's tactic of attacking Marianne by attacking women in
general has already been seen as well. For example,

(23)   Johan: I bet you'd be applauded by Women's Lib. [205]

This device is seen most strikingly in Scene Two, when Marianne and Johan return from having seen Ibsen's *A Doll's House*. Marianne liked the play; Johan didn't. Ostensibly goaded by the play, he indulges in a three-part diatribe against women, punctuated only by short and noncommittal responses from Marianne. Just a few lines from his speeches suffice to give the flavor of his comments:

(32)   Johan: (*Laughs and yawns*) Feminism is a worn-out sub-
                 ject, Marianne. Women nowadays can do what-
                 ever they like. The trouble is they can't be both-
                 ered. [68]

                                . . .

         Johan: Have you ever heard of a female symphony or-
                 chestra? Imagine a hundred and ten women with
                 menstrual trouble trying to play Rossini's over-
                 ture to "The Thieving Magpie." [69]

                                . . .

         Johan: . . . What I'd like to ask is this: Don't women
                 have a very special talent for cruelty, brutality,
                 vulgarity, and ruthlessness? . . . [70]

It is interesting to observe that this generalized attack by Johan immediately precedes the discussion about sex, in which Johan complains of Marianne's lack of interest in sex with him, and in which she again repulses his sexual advances.

An interesting aspect of Johan's and Marianne's communication system is the way in which they both continue to use only their own strategies. When Marianne uses sarcasm, Johan does not let her get away with it. For example, in Scene Three:

(33)   Johan: I don't have much self-knowledge and I under-
                 stand very little in spite of having read a lot of
                 books. But something tells me that this catastro-
                 phe is a chance in a million for both you and me.

> Marianne: Is it Paula who has put such nonsense into your
> head? Just how naive can you get?
>
> Johan: We can do without taunts and sarcastic remarks in
> this conversation.
>
> Marianne: You're right. I'm sorry. [95]

And again, in Scene Five:

(34) Johan: . . . I have to fork out a hell of a big maintenance, which incidentally I have to pay taxes on
and which is completely ruining me. So I don't see
why I should have a lot of idiotic expenses on top
of that. There's nothing to that effect in the divorce agreement, at any rate. Or is there?

Marianne: It's not the children's fault if we're worse off because you went off with another woman.

Johan: I never expected that remark from you.

Marianne: No, I'm sorry. It was crude of me. [149]

Johan's objection to Marianne's remark comes immediately after he
himself has been searingly sarcastic, just as in the preceding example.

Finally, in Scene Six, Johan delivers a long piece of philosophiz-
ing, but when Marianne responds with a small exercise in a similar
style, Johan sarcastically rebukes her.

(35) Johan: Hmm, that's the big difference between you and
me. Because I refuse to accept the complete meaninglessness behind the complete awareness. I
can't live with that cold light over all my en-
deavors. If you only knew how I struggle with my
meaninglessness. Over and over again I try to
cheer myself up by saying that life has the value
that you yourself ascribe to it. But that sort of talk
is no help to me. I want something to long for. I
want something to believe in.

Marianne: I don't feel as you do.

Johan: No. I realize that.

Marianne: Unlike you, I stick it out. And enjoy it. I rely on my common sense. And my feeling. They co-operate. I'm satisfied with both of them. Now that I'm older I have a third co-worker: my experience.

Johan: (*Gruff*) You should be a politician.

Marianne: (*Serious*) Maybe you're right. [206–207]

Let us compare Johan's and Marianne's speeches in this interchange for overall strategy and effect. His is composed of long intricate sentences, hers of short, simple ones. His words are long, Latinate, hers short and of the native vocabulary. (Here, of course, we must rely on the accuracy of the translation more than usually.) More important, he defines his situation in abstractions like "meaninglessness" and "awareness"; the value of life; "something to believe in." She, on the other hand, makes abstract concepts concrete, to the point of anthropomorphizing them: they "cooperate"; they are "co-workers." Again, he uses professional distance, she a form of childlike camaraderie. And each irritates the other. But curiously, where his posturing and pontification are finally used in the service of an admission of weakness, a plea for help (a gesture of camaraderie), her simplicity and apparent openness are used to express smug self-satisfaction, her sense that she needs nothing from him. So from the surface to the deeper levels, their strategies cross and re-cross in a most confusing design. What is perhaps even more striking, as much as each despises the other's style in the other's mouth, the recognition that the other has adopted his/her own techniques evokes strong ammunition—as with Johan in this passage, which follows (35) in the text. With increasing sarcasm (and a dose of his familiar antifemale generalization), he batters home the message that it is not appropriate for Marianne to use his strategy of smug sententiousness.

(36)   Johan: Good lord.

       Marianne: I like people. I like negotiations, prudence, compromises.

       Johan: You're practicing your election speech, I can hear it.

       Marianne: You think I'm difficult.

       Johan: Only when you preach.

       Marianne: I won't say another word.

       Johan: Promise not to tell me any more homely truths this evening?

       Marianne: I promise.

       Johan: Promise not to harp on that orgasm athlete?

       Marianne: Not another word about him.

       Johan: Do you think that *for just a little while* you can restrain your horrible sententiousness?

       Marianne: It will be difficult, but I'll try.

       Johan: Can you possibly, I say *possibly,* ration your boundless female strength?

       Marianne: I see that I'll have to.

       Johan: Come then. Let's go to bed. [207–208]

Having seen examples of Johan's and Marianne's individual uses of their separate styles, let us go on to examine how their cooperative employment of these styles works toward pragmatic identity, synonymy, and homonymy.

Pragmatic Identity

Pragmatic identity is seen when the partners use similar devices to similar ends. For example, both Johan and Marianne employ the tactic of proposing sleep when unpleasant information has been confronted. In Scene Two the couple has confronted the fact of their unsatisfactory sex life. When Marianne becomes visibly upset,

Johan says, "Let's drop this subject now and go to bed. It's late anyway." [74] In Scene Three, after Johan has told her that he is planning to leave her for another woman, Marianne adopts a similar strategy:

> (37) Johan: You know the truth now and that's the main thing.
> Marianne: I know nothing. Let's go to bed. It's late. . . . [86]

This is one variant of both Johan's and Marianne's common tactic of suggesting that a painful subject not be discussed. At the very beginning of the film, when they are interviewed for the woman's magazine, the interviewer asks Marianne her opinions about love; she becomes upset and says, "I can't see through this problem, so I'd rather not talk about it" [13]. In Scene Five, she is trying to tell Johan that they must get divorced, whereas he has changed his mind. Just when he seems to be seeing her point, she says, "Let's not talk about it" [165]. This is just what Johan says in Scene Three, after he has confronted Marianne with his plans to leave her: "We'd better not talk. There's nothing sensible to say in any case" [86]. Just as Marianne did not want to talk to the interviewer about love in marriage, Johan in Scene Five begins to tell Marianne about his unhappiness with Paula but then stops: "I can't talk about this. You know it all anyway" [161].

We have already seen that Marianne uses this strategy, too, when Johan fails to respond to her expressions of dissatisfaction in Scene Two: "You don't understand anyway, so there's no point talking about it" [45].

Pragmatic Synonymy

Pragmatic synonymy can be seen, for example, in the way Johan and Marianne avoid confrontation in Scene Three, when he returns to their country house and is about to tell her that he is leaving. Marianne deflects confrontation by excessive verbiage (Examples 15

and 16), while he does so by pontification (Example 24). The function of both their tactics is to avoid mention of the real issue: they
had a fight on the phone; she called him back and he was not at
home. Where was he, and what are the implications of that fact?
(i.e., he has a lover; he is leaving her).

Pragmatic synonymy can be seen as well in Examples 2 and 31
and the passages that precede and follow them in the dialog. Johan
and Marianne are in his office, after hours, for the purpose of sign-
ing the divorce papers. Again, they collude not to communicate, but
they do so using different pragmatic devices. This section is shown
here in full.

(38)   Johan: It's nothing but words. You put it into words so as
to placate the great emptiness. It's funny, come to
think of it. Has it ever struck you that emptiness
hurts? You'd think it might make you dizzy or
give you mental nausea. But my emptiness hurts
physically. It stings like a burn. Or like when you
were little and had been crying and the whole
inside of your body ached. I'm astonished sometimes at Paula's tremendous political faith. It's
both true and sincere and she's incessantly active
within her group. Her conviction answers her
questions and fills the emptiness. I wish I could
live as she does. I really mean it, without any
sarcasm. (*Leaning forward*) Why are you sneer-
ing? Do you think I'm talking rubbish? I think so
too as a matter of fact. But I don't care.

Marianne: I don't know what you're talking about. It seems
so theoretical. I don't know why. Perhaps because
I never talk about such big matters. I think I move
on another plane.

Johan: (*Roughly*) A more select plane, oh. A special plane
reserved for women with a privileged emotional
life and a happier, more mundane adjustment to
the mysteries of life. Paula too likes to change

> herself into a priestess of life. It's always when she
> has read a new book by some fancy preacher of
> the new women's gospel.

Marianne: I remember you always talked and talked. I used
to like it, though I hardly ever took any notice of
what you said when you held forth at your worst.
It sounds as if somewhere you were disappointed.

Johan: (*Quietly*) That's what you think.

Marianne: (*Gently*) I want you to know that I'm nearly always thinking of you and wondering if you're all
right or whether you're lonely and afraid. Every
day, several times a day, I wonder where I went
wrong. What I did to cause the breach between
us. I know it's a childish way of thinking, but
there you are. Sometimes I seem to have got hold
of the solution, then it slips through my fingers.

Johan: (*Sarcastically*) Why don't you go to a psychiatrist?
[119–120]

Johan and Marianne both try to express their sadness about the loss
of their relationship. He does so by talking in abstract generaliza-
tions ("emptiness hurts"), and by talking about finding meaning in
life, using someone else as an example (Paula, his girlfriend). Marianne does so by talking simply and directly about her own feelings
for him. She also blames herself and puts herself down. In both
cases, the other refuses to "hear" the other's message. Marianne
denies the validity of what Johan says; she dismisses his concerns
("I never talk about such big matters") as irrelevant and proclaims
her own domain of feelings ("I move on another plane"). Johan
dismisses Marianne's expression of feelings with sarcasm ("Why
don't you go to a psychiatrist"). In response to Marianne's refusal to
respond to his admission of loneliness, he again uses sarcasm and
the device of attacking her as a woman. Marianne's response to this
is to redouble her tactic of dismissing what he says as irrelevant and
again to bring the conversation to the area of feelings, and of him
personally ("It sounds as if somewhere you were disappointed").

Pragmatic Homonymy

To create pragmatic homonymy, Marianne and Johan use the same surface devises to achieve different ends. For example, both Johan and Marianne employ barrages of questions. As we saw earlier, Marianne greets Johan at their country house with a barrage of questions offering him different types of food. In the same episode, Example 15, she utters a string of rhetorical questions in which she invokes "a better life." While these questions have the apparent intent of inviting camaraderie (by requiring a response, they seem to involve the partner in the communication), their underlying effect is distance, served by avoiding the real problems between them. Still another time, Marianne uses a barrage of questions to avoid hearing answers to any one of them:

(39) Marianne: Do you want a divorce? Are you going to marry her? Anyway, why do you have to tell me about this tonight of all times? Why the sudden hurry? [85]

By asking the follow-up questions, Marianne prevents Johan's answering the first, real ones.

Johan also asks a barrage of questions, but his are rhetorical, and their function is quite different:

(40) Johan: Do you know how long I've had this in mind? Can you guess? I don't mean about Paula, but about leaving you and the children and our home. Can you guess? [88]

Johan's rhetorical questions take the form of taunts. Similarly, he mocks Marianne's style by asking a barrage of questions which are purported to reveal what she is thinking:

(41) Marianne: . . . You're putting me in a ridiculous and intolerable position. Surely you can see that.

> Johan: I know just what you mean: What are our parents
> going to say? What will my sister think, what will
> our friends think? Jesus Christ, how tongues are
> going to wag! How will it affect the girls, and
> what will their school friends' mothers think? And
> what about the dinner parties we're invited to in
> September and October? And what are you going
> to say to Katarina and Peter? . . . [91]

While Johan's questions have the apparent intent of distance—by
their sarcasm, they can only drive Marianne further from him—yet
they work toward a deeper effect of camaraderie, by drawing her
into emotional interaction. Taunts can only rouse Marianne to anger and therefore to involvement.

THE USE OF QUESTIONS

To see still more clearly how this couple's verbal strategies operate
on these multiple levels, we can examine the use of questions in
Scene Three, the scene in which Johan returns to the country home
and announces that he will leave. In sheer numbers, Marianne asks
nearly twice as many questions as Johan: 63 to his 37. If questions
are the linguistic form that seeks to involve the interlocutor by
necessitating a response, then Marianne shows herself to be seeking
involvement through her greater use of questions. It is even more
revealing, however, to examine the types of questions they ask.
Overwhelmingly, Marianne asks real questions while Johan asks
rhetorical ones. Of her 63 questions, 50 are real; that is, they ask for
information in most cases, and in some cases for a response (for
example, "Can't you help me with this?" [92]). Thirteen of Marianne's questions are rhetorical: i.e., no response is expected. In
other words, 21 percent of Marianne's questions are rhetorical,
while 79 percent are real. In contrast, of Johan's 37 questions, 32 (86
percent) are rhetorical, and 5 (14 percent) are real.

Although the purpose of Marianne's questions seems to be to

keep Johan involved with her, the only questions that succeed in eliciting talk from him are those that seek information about his relationship with Paula; therefore Marianne asks one after another of these. In addition, she uses the indirect device of offering assistance in question form:

(42) Marianne: Shall we pack now or have breakfast first? Would you like tea or coffee, by the way? [98]

· · ·

Marianne: Shall I pack the shaver, or will you take the one you have in town?

· · ·

Marianne: Do you want the receipt for the dry cleaners?

· · ·

Marianne: . . . Which pyjamas are you taking? [99]

Johan, in contrast, does not ask for help in question form, but uses simple imperatives or declaratives.

(43) Johan: Help me, please. I've a split nail and can't manage it. [98]

While Marianne uses information questions to draw Johan into the interaction by getting him to talk about himself, Johan's five real questions do not function in this way. Three of those five real questions seek information about his belongings:

(44) Johan: Do you know if my gray suit is here or in town? [86]

· · ·

Johan: Do you know what has become of Speer's memoirs? I'm sure I left the book on the bedside table. [98]

· · ·

Johan: . . . Which cleaners is it? [99]

These questions remind Marianne of her involvement with Johan, but it is the involvement of caretaking, of household management. In contrast, Marianne tries, through questions, to involve Johan in a personal way. Whereas in Scene Two he was sexually interested in her and she avoided his advances, in this scene she tries to interest him sexually but he does not respond. For example, after her flight of fancy about Aunt Miriam and Uncle David, she asks suddenly,

(45) Marianne: Shall I take my curlers out? [83]

This seems like an invitation to bed, to make herself more sexually attractive as a prelude to lovemaking. However, Johan fends off the proposition:

(46)   Johan: Don't mind me. [84]

Similarly, early in the scene, she tries to elicit a remark from him about her body, but meets with similar lack of interest:

(47) Marianne: . . . I've lost over four pounds this last week.
               Does it show?
        Johan: No. [83]

Johan and Marianne both make much use of questions but though their utterances may appear superficially alike, they have different communicative intentions or meanings. His questions are rhetorical, superficially designed to repulse further interchanges. On the surface they are hostile, and provoke distance. Superficially, Marianne's questions look like Johan's: a question is a question. But in intent—the consciously-perceived intent of the speaker, insofar as the audience can make assumptions about it—her questions are asked in search of information. Unlike Johan's, they are asked with the expectation of eliciting a reply. They are designed to invite camaraderie.

But in fact, at a still deeper level, not accessible to the participants themselves, the level at which we determine the effect of others' utterances on ourselves, the strategies match once more. While Johan's questions preclude surface interaction, they create continuing involvement by arousing anger, perceptibly or not. (If Johan merely withdrew, the effect would be truly distancing.) Marianne, that is, perceives and responds to Johan's distancing questions as if they were camaraderie-creating, as hers are: she understands his contributions in terms of what they would mean if they were hers. (This is a general principle of discourse, that we can understand the contributions of others only in terms of what we would mean by producing them.) But they shut off true communication by creating anger. Marianne rises to the challenge, and is moved by his diatribes to respond with ever more furious spates of information-seeking questions and offers of help. Although these are, superficially, camaraderie-inviting, Johan's skill in fending them off, coupled with their very intensity, guarantee that they will not create interaction—that they will stifle it. Johan perceives her questions as barrier-creating devices—as, ultimately, they are, in effect. So Johan's and Marianne's strategies match at the level of surface form; conflict at the level of deeper intent; but match once more at the deepest and least accessible level, that of the effect on the other participant; and the ultimate effect of the couple's communicative strategies is complicity—an implicit agreement or metastrategy to avoid real communication. These intertwinings are represented as follows:

SURFACE	Johan and Marianne both ask questions	MATCH
DEEPER LEVEL: *(Speaker's intent)*	Johan's questions are distancing; Marianne's questions generate rapport	CONFLICT
DEEPEST LEVEL: *(Effect on Addressee)*	Johan's and Marianne's stylistic differences create shared implicit strategy: noncommunication	MATCH

The complicity at the deepest level underlying the dissension between Johan and Marianne is a key to the general plot of the series. At first glance, it is puzzling that these two apparently so compatible people should have to separate; but after a while, what becomes still more curious is that these two people who apparently are continually at odds with each other cannot stay apart. We who watch feel that it makes sense—we know relationships like this—but offhand it seems merely paradoxical, one of the inexplicable mysteries of human psychology. But if we disentangle Johan's and Marianne's communicative strategies thoroughly enough, the mystery turns out to be quite predictable.

Johan and Marianne become quite aware of their surface discord and, somewhat more dimly, of their deeper stylistic incompatibility. What they do not see is their essential complicity at the deepest level: their implicit agreement to disagree. Because of that underlying and overriding similarity of intent and desire, this couple actually has a great deal in common. It may not make for pleasant or productive communication, but the similarity creates a need, and an indissoluble bond between them. As long as they both are in this close bond, they cannot break apart. But as long as they are operating under different assumptions about what constitutes an effective or appropriate contribution, they will create friction between them with everything they say.

The levels of cooperation and conflict create a sort of paradoxical communicative situation: people can operate in complicity by talking at apparent cross-purposes, and an understanding of their communicative strategies is only possible through a recognition of this paradox. What is apparently conflict-ridden and anticommunicative is in effect deeply satisfying to the participants.

The situation in *Scenes from a Marriage,* then, has overtones of the Batesonian double bind (Bateson 1972) in which a paradoxical communicative strategy keeps participants from fulfilling their communicative needs. A double bind, however, is by Bateson's definition unilateral: it is effected from above by an authority who himself or herself remains free. But the situation here, while it has certain aspects of the double bind, is bilateral: it is arrived at by negotiation by both participants, both derive equal benefit, and it can be resolved by both participants together. In this way, while it creates confusion and conflict in its participants, it is not pathogenic in the way the double bind is.

This examination of one couple's interaction pattern suggests, tentatively, a general hypothesis: these alternations of match and conflict are typical of couples that are intermeshed like Johan and Marianne, who can neither live together compatibly nor separate cleanly. A truly harmonious relationship (supposing this is more than a mythical construct) would entail matchings at all levels; a clearly discordant one, conflict at all levels. It is this intermediate type that is problematic for its users, as well as being most interesting to theorists of communication. (For instance, see Watzlawick, Beavin, and Jackson 1967 for a different but related view of troubled interaction.)

CONCLUSION

In this chapter, taking *Scenes from a Marriage* as a text, we have suggested both a new methodology for interpreting communication and a new development of a theory of communicative competence. We have argued that the examination of a constructed text enables us to inspect pragmatic competence—speakers' abstract knowledge of what is expected of them in a discourse. We have also given some evidence of the complexity of communicative strategies and the number of factors participants are operating with. We show that pragmatic structures, like those elsewhere in grammar, entail a multi-leveled analysis, from superficially accessible to deep and implicit, and that contributions of different participants can be related to each other in terms of their functioning as pragmatic paraphrases, ambiguities, or identities. We argue finally on this basis that the choice of forms and the effects of these forms can only be understood with reference to these levels, and that both the structure of a single conversation and the pattern of an entire relationship is explicable in terms of the matchings and conflicts among the consciously accessible and deeper levels of the participants' conversational strategies.

NOTES

This chapter originally appeared in *Semiotica* 49:3/4(1984).323–346. The authors are grateful to David Gordon and Marcia Perlstein for helpful discussion, suggestions, and criticism. Additionally, the paper by Friedrich and Redfield (1978) has been a source of inspiration to us as an example of the use of linguistic theory to illuminate our responses to characters in literature. An earlier and shorter version of this paper appeared in Proceedings of the Fifth Annual Meeting of the Berkeley Linguistic Society (1979). The subheadings were added here to enhance readability.

1. See Tannen (1984) for an extended analysis of conversational style, with data from natural conversation.

2. It may be objected that the fact that *Scenes from a Marriage* is accessible to us only in translation invalidates it for the purpose of close textual analysis. Certainly this is a serious issue, but it is difficult to be sure how, or how seriously, the fact of its being a translation affects its utility to us. It is probable that no significant problems would arise on the word-by-word, or even sentence-by-sentence level; however, we might wonder, for instance, whether a question in Swedish had the same pragmatic effect as its English counterpart. Tannen (1981, reprinted in this volume) has shown that questions do not necessarily have the same pragmatic effect for contemporary Greeks and Americans, nor even necessarily for members of the same linguistic community. Since abstract problems like this have not been discussed in the literature on translation, we must leave this theoretically valid and fascinating question open and hope for the best. But the American audience's recognition of the validity of the dialog seems to indicate that there is no serious difficulty.

3. Ingmar Bergman, *Scenes from a Marriage,* translated by Alan Blair. New York: Bantam (1974), p. 26. Subsequent page references appear in brackets in the text. Spaced dots show ellipsis. Unspaced dots are a form of punctuation that appears in the original.

REFERENCES

Bateson, Gregory (1972). *Steps to an Ecology of Mind.* New York: Ballantine.
Friedrich, Paul, and James Redfield (1978). Speech as a personality symbol: The case of Achilles. *Language* 54, 263–88.
Lakoff, Robin Tolmach (1979). Stylistic strategies within a grammar of style. *Annals of the New York Academy of Sciences* 327, 53–78.
Tannen, Deborah (1981). Indirectness in discourse: Ethnicity as conversational

style. *Discourse Processes* 4:3.221–38. Reprinted in this volume as Ethnic style in male–female conversation.

Tannen, Deborah (1984). *Conversational style: Analyzing talk among friends.* Norwood, NJ: Ablex.

Watzlawick, Paul, Janet Beavin, and Don D. Jackson (1967). *Pragmatics of Human Communication.* New York: Norton.

CHAPTER FIVE

Ethnic Style in
Male–Female Conversation

This chapter, my first on the topic of gender and language, presents a radically different methodological approach from the other chapters included in the present volume and my other work. It is similar, however, to much of my other work in its concerns: misunderstandings resulting from style differences, indirectness in conversation, and a comparison of Greek and American conversational strategies. (Other works in which I examine modern Greek discourse include Tannen 1980, 1983, 1984b, 1986; Tannen and Kakava 1992; Tannen and Oztek 1981.) However, instead of directly interpreting the discourse examples, in this study I examined patterns of interpretation of a sample conversation by distributing questionnaires to a number of respondents who are members of three groups: Greeks, Americans, and Greek-Americans. (The total number of respondents [82] is large by comparison to the case-study approach typical of interpretive sociolinguistics but small by the standards of statistical surveys.) Counting the number of respondents who chose one or another interpretation of sample conversations (conversations which may sound familiar to readers of my book That's Not What I Meant!: How Conversational Style Makes or Breaks Your Relations With Others) *revealed a pattern by which the three groups fell along a continuum, with Greeks the most likely to choose an indirect interpretation, Americans the least likely, and Greek-Americans in between somewhat closer to the Greeks. Separating the groups into male and female respondents indicated little difference between Greek and Greek-American men and women, but slightly more American women than men chose the indirect interpretation. Suggestive as these findings are, it is really impossible to conclude anything from these numbers because they are so small.*

More revealing, therefore, is the pattern of comments made by respondents when they were asked to explain their choices and offer alternative linguistic forms that would have led them to make the other choice. Among the results of this qualitative section of the study is what I call an "enthusiasm constraint," by which Greeks found the response "O.K." to be an indirect way to say "no" because it lacks enthusiasm. Related to this is what I called the "brevity effect": There were both Greeks and Americans who made reference to the brevity of the response "OK," but those Americans who did so mentioned brevity as an explanation for choosing the direct *interpretation; they explained that brevity indicates casualness and therefore sincerity. In contrast, those Greeks who referred to the brevity of "OK" did so to explain why they chose the* indirect *interpretation; they explained that brevity indicates a lack of enthusiasm and therefore an unwillingness to comply with another's perceived preferences. The responses of Greek-Americans were a blend of the typical Greek and typical American responses.*

This chapter is more directly concerned with issues of cultural variation and patterns of indirectness than with gender differences, but it examines these issues in the context of examples of male–female communication. I include it in this volume not only in order to provide a comprehensive view of my work on gender and language but, more important, because the cross-cultural perspective is a crucial element that must be borne in mind when addressing issues of gender-related variation.

THIS CHAPTER FOCUSES ON indirectness in male–female discourse, seen as a feature of conversational style. The present analysis investigates social, rather than individual, differences in the context of conversation between married partners; however, the phenomena elucidated operate in individual style as well. Investigation of expectations of indirectness by Greeks, Americans, and Greek-Americans traces the process of adaptation of this conversational strategy as an element of ethnicity.

Misunderstandings due to different uses of indirectness are commonplace among members of what appear to (but may not necessarily) be the same culture. However, such mixups are particularly characteristic of cross-cultural communication. There are individual as well as social differences with respect to what is deemed appropriate to say and how it is deemed appropriate to say it.

It is sharing of conversational strategies that creates the feeling of satisfaction which accompanies and follows successful conversation: the sense of being understood, being "on the same wave length," belonging, and therefore of sharing identity. Conversely, a lack of congruity in conversational strategies creates the opposite feeling: of dissonance, not being understood, not belonging and therefore of not sharing identity. This is the sense in which conversational style is a major component of what we have come to call ethnicity.

Conversational control processes operate on an automatic level. While it is commonly understood that different languages or different dialects have different words for the same object, in contrast, ways of signalling intentions and attitudes seem self-evident, natural, and real.

Much recent linguistic research has been concerned with the fact that interpretation of utterances in conversation often differs radically from the meaning that would be derived from the sentences in isolation. Robin Lakoff (1973) observes that sociocultural goals, broadly called *politeness,* lead people to express opinions and preferences in widely varying linguistic forms. Lakoff's (1979) recent work demonstrates that characteristic choices with respect to indirectness give rise to personal style, and that an individual's style is a mixture of strategies which shift in response to shifting situations. Ervin-Tripp (1976) has shown the great variation in surface form which directives may take in American English. Brown and Levinson ([1978]1987) argue that the form taken by utterances in actual interaction can be seen as the linguistic means of satisfying the coexisting and often conflicting needs for *negative face* (the need to be left alone) and *positive face* (the need to be approved of by others). As a result, people often prefer to express their wants and opinions *off record*—that is, indirectly.

Indirectness is a necessary means for serving the needs for *rapport* and *defensiveness,* associated respectively with Brown and Levinson's positive and negative face. *Rapport* is the lovely satisfaction of being understood without explaining oneself, of getting what one wants without asking for it. *Defensiveness* is the need to be able to save face by reneging in case one's conversational contribution is not received well—the ability to say, perhaps sincerely, "I never said that," or "That isn't what I meant." The goals of rapport and defensiveness correspond to Lakoff's politeness rules "Maintain camaraderie" and "Don't impose."

An individual learns conversational strategies in previous interactive experience, but chooses certain and rejects other strategies made available in this way. In other words, the range of strategies familiar to a speaker is socially determined, but any individual's set of habitual strategies is unique within that range. For example, research has shown that New Yorkers of Jewish background often use overlap—that is, simultaneous talk—in a cooperative way; many members of this group talk simultaneously in some settings without intending to interrupt (Tannen 1984, chapter 2). This does not imply that all New Yorkers of Jewish background use overlap cooperatively. However, a speaker of this background is more likely to do so than someone raised in the Midwest. And it is even more unlikely that such simultaneous talk will be used by an Athabaskan raised in Alaska, according to the findings of Scollon (1985), who has shown that Athabaskans highly value silence and devalue what they perceive as excessive talk.

The present analysis and discussion seeks to investigate social differences in expectations of indirectness in certain contexts by Greeks, Americans, and Greek-Americans, tracing the process of adaptation of this conversational strategy as an element of ethnicity. The research design is intended to identify patterns of interpretation, not to predict the styles of individual members of these groups.

INDIRECTNESS IN DISCOURSE

A Greek woman of about 65 told me that, before she married, she had to ask her father's permission before doing anything. She noted that of course he never explicitly denied her permission. If she asked, for example, whether she could go to a dance, and he answered,

(1)   An thes, pas. (If you want, you can go.)

she knew that she could not go. If he really meant that she could go, he would say,

(2)   Ne. Na pas. (Yes. You should go.)

The intonation in (1) rises on the conditional clause, creating a tentative effect, while the intonation in (2) falls twice in succession, resulting in an assertive effect. This informant added that her husband responds to her requests in the same way. Thus she agrees to do what he prefers without expecting him to express his preference directly.

This example is of a situation in which interlocutors share expectations about how intentions are to be communicated; their communication is thus successful. To investigate processes of indirectness, however, it is useful to focus on interactions in which communication is not successful (Gumperz and Tannen 1979). Such sequences are the discourse equivalents of starred sentences in syntactic argumentation. They render apparent processes which go unnoticed when communication is successful.

The present chapter focuses on communication between married partners. Interactions between couples reveal the effects of differing uses of indirectness over time. People often think that couples who live together and love each other must come to understand each other's conversational styles. However, research has shown that repeated interaction does not necessarily lead to better understanding. On the contrary, it may reinforce mistaken judgments of the other's intentions and increase expectations that the other will behave as before. If differing styles led to the earlier impression that the partner is stubborn, irrational, or uncooperative, similar behavior is expected to continue. This has been shown for group contact among Greeks and Americans (Vassiliou, Triandis, Vassiliou, and McGuire 1972) and can be seen in personal relations as well. Misjudgment is calcified by the conviction of repeated experience.

Systematic study of comparative communicative strategies was made by asking couples about experiences in which they became aware of differing interpretations of conversations. It became clear that certain types of communication were particularly given to misinterpretation—requests, excuses, explanation: in short, verbalizations associated with getting one's way. One couple recalled a typical argument in which both maintained that they had not gone to a party because the other had not wanted to go. Each partner denied having expressed any disinclination to go. A misunderstand -

ing such as this might well go undetected between casual acquaintances, but, between couples, ongoing interaction makes it likely that such differences will eventually surface.

In this case, the mixup was traced to the following reconstructed conversations:

(3)   Wife: John's having a party. Wanna go?
    Husband: OK.
    (Later)
      Wife: Are you sure you want to go to the party?
    Husband: OK, let's not go. I'm tired anyway.

In this example the wife was an American native New Yorker of East European Jewish extraction. It is likely that this background influenced her preference for a seemingly direct style. (This phenomenon among speakers of this background is the focus of analysis in Tannen 1981, 1984.) In discussing the misunderstanding, the American wife reported she had merely been asking what her husband wanted to do without considering her own preference. Since she was about to go to this party just for him, she tried to make sure that that was his preference by asking him a second time. She was being solicitous and considerate. The Greek husband said that by bringing up the question of the party, his wife was letting him know that she wanted to go, so he agreed to go. Then when she brought it up again, she was letting him know that she didn't want to go; she had obviously changed her mind. So he came up with a reason not to go, to make her feel all right about getting her way. This is precisely the strategy reported by the Greek woman who did what her father or husband wanted without expecting them to tell her directly what that was. Thus the husband in example 3 was also being solicitous and considerate. All this considerateness, however, only got them what neither wanted, because they were expecting to receive information differently from the way the other was sending it out.

A key to understanding the husband's strategy is his use of

"OK." To the wife, "OK" was a positive response, in free variation with other positive responses such as "yes" or "yeah." In addition, his use of *anyway* is an indication that he agrees. Finally, the husband's intonation, tone of voice, and nonverbal signals such as facial expression and kinesics would have contributed to the impact of his message. Nonetheless, the wife asserted that, much as she could see the reasoning behind such interpretations in retrospect, she still missed the significance of these cues at the time. The key, I believe, is that she was not expecting to receive her husband's message through subtle cues; she was assuming he would tell her what he wanted to do directly. To the listener, a misunderstanding is indistinguishable from an understanding; one commits to an interpretation and proceeds to fit succeeding information into that mold. People will put up with a great deal of seemingly inappropriate verbal behavior before questioning the line of interpretation which seems self-evident. Direct questioning about how a comment was meant is likely to be perceived as a challenge or criticism.

This example demonstrates, furthermore, the difficulty of clearing up misunderstandings caused by stylistic differences. In seeking to clarify, each speaker continues to use the very strategy that confused the other in the first place. In this way, interaction often results in increasing divergence rather than convergence of style. That is, each partner's characteristic style leads the other to apply increasingly extreme forms of the conflicting strategy. In example 3, the wife's strategy for clarifying was to go "on record," through a direct question, as inquiring about her husband's preference, and to ask her husband to go on record about his preference. Since the husband did not expect preferences to be directly expressed, his wife's second question seemed to him an even more recondite hint. He responded with an even more subtle use of indirectness: to allow her to get her way and to offer a reason of his own in justification. And so it goes. Expectations about how meaning will be communicated are so compelling that information intended in a different mode is utterly opaque.

A key parameter here is setting. Does a participant define an interaction as one in which it is appropriate to hint? Numerous discussions triggered by the presentation of these findings have suggested possible male–female differences among Americans in this regard. An audience member commented, "When I first started going out with my boyfriend, we never had misunderstandings about where we should go and what we should do. Now that we've been going together for two years, it seems to happen all the time. How come?" My hypothesis is that, at the beginning of their acquaintance, both partners deemed it appropriate to watch out for the other's hints, to give options. However, as the relationship was redefined, the woman expected increased use of indirectness, reasoning, "We know each other so well, you will know what I want without my telling you." The man, on the other hand, expected less indirectness, reasoning, "We know each other so well that we can tell each other what we want." As the context of their relationship changed, they differed in how they expected their communicative strategies to change. In addition, when partners interact over time, they become more rather than less likely to react, perhaps negatively, to each other's subtle cues, as repeated experience leads them to expect such behavior.

Another example of a reported conversation between a married couple follows.

(4)   Husband: Let's go visit my boss tonight.
       Wife: Why?
       Husband: All right, we don't have to go.

Both husband and wife agreed that the husband's initial proposal was an indication that he wanted to visit his boss. However, they disagreed on the meaning of the wife's question, "Why?" The wife explained that she meant it as a request for information. Therefore she was confused and frustrated and couldn't help wondering why she married such an erratic man who suddenly changed his mind only a moment after making a request. The husband, for his part, explained that his wife's question clearly meant that she did not want to go, and he therefore rescinded his request. He was frustrated, however, and resentful of her for refusing. In discussion, the wife, who was American, reported that she systematically confronted this strange reaction to her asking "Why?" Certainly, the use of this question can be either a request for information or an indirect way of stalling or resisting compliance with a perceived request. The key here is which meaning of "why" is likely to be used in this context.

CULTURALLY RELATIVE PATTERNS OF INTERPRETATION: A PILOT STUDY

In order to determine to what extent cross-cultural differences are operating in patterns of interpretation of indirectness, further systematic questioning of Greeks, Americans, and Greek-Americans was undertaken. The remainder of this chapter reports results of that research.

The Greek sample was taken from native Greeks living in the Bay Area of California. Most were young men who had come to the United States for graduate study or women contacted through church organizations. Therefore the age and educational levels differed sharply for men and women. In all cases, Greek respondents had been exposed to American communicative systems. That differences emerged nonetheless is a testament to the reality of the effect.

Greek-Americans were contacted in New York City because it was not possible to find California Greek-Americans who had grown up in distinctly Greek communities. The fact that Greek-Americans from New York are compared with Americans from California is now seen as a weakness; subsequent research (Tannen 1984) has indicated that New Yorkers are less likely to expect indirectness than Californians. Again, the fact that differences do emerge is testimony to the effect of ethnicity. Finally, Americans with Greek-born parents and grandparents are lumped together in this study. There is some indication that those with Greek parents show the effect of ethnicity more strongly than do those of Greek grandparents and American-born parents.

A questionnaire was designed to present the Greek, American, and Greek-American respondents with the conversation about going to a party. The questionnaire elicited their interpretations by presenting paraphrase choices and then asked for explanations of those choices in order to identify the interpretive strategies motivating them. The first part of the questionnaire reads:

(5) A couple had the following conversation:

> Wife: John's having a party. Wanna go?
>
> Husband: OK.
>
> Wife: I'll call and tell him we're coming.

Based on this conversation only, put a check next to the statement which you think explains what the husband really meant when he answered "OK."

> [1–I] My wife wants to go to this party, since she asked. I'll go to make her happy.
>
> [1–D] My wife is asking if I want to go to a party. I feel like going, so I'll say yes.

What is it about the way the wife and the husband spoke, that gave you that impression?

What would the wife or husband have had to have said differently, in order for you to have checked the other statement?

The first choice, here referred to as 1–I (Indirect), represents roughly what the Greek husband reported he had meant by "OK." 1–D (Direct) represents what the American wife reported she had thought he meant. A comparison of the percentage of respondents in the three groups who opted for Paraphrase 1–I turns out looking much like a continuum, with Greeks the most likely to take the indirect interpretation, Americans the least likely, and Greek-Americans in the middle, somewhat closer to Greeks (see table 1).

Table 1. *Respondents Choosing 1–I*

Greeks (27)	Greek-Americans (30)	Americans (25)
48%	43%	32%
(13)	(13)	(8)

In example 5, and throughout the present discussion, I refer to one interpretation as direct and the other as indirect. These labels reflect the two possible functions of the question: as a request for information (its literal sense) and as an off-record show of resistance (an indirect speech act). This is not to imply, however, that anyone's conversational style is categorically direct. In a sense, all interpretation in context is indirect. What are variable are the modes of indirectness—when and how it is deemed appropriate to hint, that is, to signal unstated contextual and interpersonal information.

It has been suggested (Lakoff 1975) that American women tend to be more indirect than American men. As seen in tables 2 and 3, percentages of respondents taking the indirect interpretation are more or less the same for Greek men and women and for Greek-American men and women, while, for Americans, separating male and female respondents yields quite different percentages, with

Table 2. *Male Respondents Choosing 1–I*

Greeks (10)	Greek-Americans (9)	Americans (11)
50%	44%	27%
(5)	(4)	(3)

Table 3. *Female Respondents Choosing 1–I*

Greeks (17)	Greek-Americans (21)	Americans (14)
47%	43%	36%
(8)	(9)	(5)

fewer men and more women choosing Paraphrase 1–I. If these samples are representative, they are intriguing in suggesting a stylistic gulf between American men and women which does not exist between Greek men and women.

The second part of the questionnaire presents the second part of the conversation, followed by paraphrase choice and questions about interpretive strategies. It reads:

(6) Later, the same couple had this conversation:

> Wife: Are you sure you want to go to the party?

> Husband: OK, let's not go. I'm tired anyway.

Based on *both* conversations which you read, put a check next to the statement that you think explains what the husband really meant when he spoke the second time:

[2–I] It sounds like my wife doesn't really want to go, since she's asking about it again. I'll say I'm tired, so we don't have to go, and she won't feel bad about preventing me from going.

[2–D] Now that I think about it again, I don't really feel like going to a party because I'm tired.

> What is it about the way the husband or wife spoke that gave you that impression?

> What would they have had to have said differently, in order for you to have checked the other statement?

The two paraphrases presented in the second part of the questionnaire represent the respective interpretations reported by the Greek husband (the one here labeled 2–I, Indirect) and the American wife (here labeled 2–D, Direct) in the actual interchange. This also highlights an aspect of the questionnaire which is different for male and female respondents. Women and men are both asked to interpret the husband's comments, while it is likely that women identify with the wife and men with the husband. Furthermore, the indirect interpretation is favored by the fact that the husband's response indicates that he took that interpretation.

Table 4. *Respondents Choosing 1–I and 2–I*

Greeks (27)	Greek-Americans (30)	Americans (25)
26%	20%	12%
(7)	(6)	(3)

The choice of both 1–I and 2–I reveals the most indirect interpretive strategy, by which both the wife's questions are taken to indicate her hidden preferences—or at least that the husband's reply is taken to show that he interprets them that way. Again, results fall out on a continuum, with Greeks the most likely to take the indirect interpretation, Americans the least likely, and Greek-Americans in between, slightly closer to the Greeks (see table 4).

Quantitative results, then, tended to corroborate the impression that more Greeks than Americans opted for the indirect interpretation of questions, and that Greek-Americans were in between, slightly closer to Greeks. However, the pilot study questionnaire was not designed primarily to yield quantitative data. The main function of the paraphrase choices was to serve as a basis for short answers and extended discussion about the patterns of interpretation which prompted one or the other choice, and the linguistic and contextual factors influencing them. Results of the short answer and interview/discussion components follow.

Patterns of Interpretation: Qualitative Results

Patterns of interpretation emerged from respondents' explanations of their choice of paraphrase and from alternative linguistic forms they reported would have led them to the other choice. Following paraphrase choices, the questionnaire asked, "What is it about the way the wife and the husband spoke that gave you that impression?" and then, "What would the wife or husband have had to have said differently in order for you to have checked the other statement?" Differences in explanations of interpretations were systematic in reference to two aspects of the conversation: the wife's asking of questions, and the form of the husband's responses.

Paraphrase 1–I indicates that the wife's question means she wants to go to the party. The reasoning reported by Greeks to explain their choice of 1–I is that if the wife didn't want to go, she would not have brought it up in the first place. Greeks, Americans, and probably members of any cultural group are capable of interpreting a question either as a request for information or as an expression of some unstated meaning. However, members of one culture or another may be more likely to interpret a question in a particular context in one way or another. Much recent research in pragmatics has elaborated on the indirect speech act function of questions as requests for action, or commands. Esther Goody (1978:40) set out to discover why natives of Gonja do not ask questions in teaching and learning situations. She concluded that Gonjans are "trained early on to attend above all to the command function of questioning. The pure information question hasn't got a chance!" Similarly, I suggest, in the context under consideration, natives of Greece are more disposed to attend to the indirect request function of questions.

Respondents' comments explaining why they chose one or the other paraphrase often focused on the husband's choice of OK. Americans who thought the husband really wanted to go to the party explained that OK = yes (24 percent of the Americans said this). But if they thought the husband was going along with his wife's preference, the Americans still focused on "OK" as the cue. In this case they explained that "OK" lacks enthusiasm (20 percent of the Americans said this).

The expectation of enthusiasm was stronger for Greeks than for Americans. Whereas 24 percent of the Americans pointed to the affirmative nature of "OK," not a single Greek did so. In contrast, fully half of the Greeks who explained their choices referred to the fact that "OK" (in Greek, *endaxi*) was an unenthusiastic response. This is more than double the percentage of Americans (20 percent) who said this. The *enthusiasm constraint* is in keeping with findings of Vassiliou, Triandis, Vassiliou and McGuire (1972), who conclude that Greeks place value on enthusiasm and spontaneity (as opposed to American emphasis on planning and organization). Vassiliou et al. observe that such differences in "subjective culture" may contribute to the formation of ethnic stereotypes.

Related to the enthusiasm constraint—perhaps another aspect of it—is the *brevity effect.* Many respondents referred to the brevity of the husband's response when they explained their paraphrase choices. However, if Americans made reference to his brevity, it was in explanation of their choice of paraphrase 1–D, the direct interpretation. Their reasoning was that brevity evidenced informality, casualness, and hence sincerity. This explanation is based on a strategy which assumes that people will express preferences directly in this context. More than a quarter (28 percent) of the American respondents took this approach. In stark contrast, any Greeks who mentioned the brevity of the husband's answer "OK" (*endaxi*), pointed to it as evidence that he was reluctant to go to the party. To them, brevity is a sign of unwillingness to comply with another's perceived preference. This interpretation presupposes that resistance to another's preference, in this context, will not be verbalized directly; 20 percent of Greek respondents took this approach.[1]

The explanations given by Greek-Americans for their paraphrase choices were a blend of typical Greek and typical American explanations. They explained that brevity reveals lack of enthusiasm, whereas no Americans did, and they explained that brevity is casual, whereas no Greeks did, in roughly the same proportions (23 percent and 20 percent, respectively). Only two (7 percent said that OK = yes, whereas no Greeks and 24 percent of Americans said this. Thus Greek-Americans were closer to Greeks than to Americans in their interpretive style.

Further corroborative results came in the form of comments volunteered by respondents following their completion of the questionnaire; the suggestion that Greeks tend to be more indirect in the context of an intimate relationship "rang true" for respondents.

What are the implications of such differences for cross-cultural communication? It is possible that a good bicultural, like a good bilingual, sees both possibilities and code-switches. For example, an American-born woman of Greek grandparents said that she had to check both paraphrases on the questionnaire. She explained that if she projected herself into the position of the wife, she would take the indirect interpretation, but if she imagined her non-Greek husband asking, she would take the direct paraphrase. In other words, she was aware of both possible strategies. She commented that she tends to be indirect because she picked it up from her mother, who was influenced by her own mother (i.e., the grandmother born in Greece). In the same spirit, another Greek-American woman laughed when she read paraphrase 2–I, saying, "That sounds just like my grandmother."

It is far from certain, however, that awareness of the existence of differences in communicative strategies makes them less troublesome, since their operation remains unconscious and habitual. Again, a personal testimony is most eloquent: that of a professional man living in New York City, whose grandparents were from Greece. He seemed fully assimilated, did not speak Greek, had not been raised in a Greek neighborhood, and had few Greek friends. In filling out the questionnaire, he chose paraphrase 1–I, the initial indirect interpretation. In later discussion he said that the notion of indirectness "rang such a bell." He commented, ". . . to a great extent being Greek implies a certain feeling of differentness with regard to understanding others which I have some trouble with." He elaborated on what he meant: "I was trying to get at the idea of . . . this very thing that we talked about [indirectness] and I see it as either something heroically different or a real impediment . . . Most of the time I think of it as a problem. And I can't really sort it out from my family and background . . . I don't know if it's Greek. I just know that it's me. And it feels a little better to know that it's Greek."

CONCLUSION

These results indicate how respondents report they would interpret a conversation. In actual interaction, intonation, facial expression, past experience with these and other speakers, and a myriad other factors influence interpretation. Moreover, whenever people communicate, they convey not only the content of their message, but an image of themselves (Goffman 1959). Thus respondents must have referred for their answers not only to their interactive experience but also to their notion of social norms.

Eventually such an approach must be combined with tape-recording and video-taping of actual interaction, to determine not only what speakers expect but what they do.

Conversational style—the ways it seems natural to express and interpret meaning in conversation—is learned through communicative experience and therefore is influenced by family communicative habits. As the Greek-American quoted above put it, one "can't really sort it out from family and background." In other words, conversational style is both a consequence and indicator of ethnicity. Conversational style includes both how meaning is expressed, as seen in patterns of indirectness, and what meaning is expressed, as in how much enthusiasm is expected. All of these conversational strategies create impressions about the speaker—judgments which are made, ultimately, not about how one talks but about what kind of person one is. Conversational style, therefore, has much to do with the formation of ethnic stereotypes.

Conversational style is more resistant to change than more apparent marks of ethnicity such as retention of the parents' or grandparents' language. Seaman (1972:204) demonstrates that the modern Greek language is "practically extinct" among third generation Greek-Americans and will be "totally extinct in the fourth generation." However, those very third generation Greek-Americans who have lost the Greek language may not have lost, or not lost entirely, Greek communicative strategies. Understanding these strategies, and the patterns of their retention or loss, can offer insight into the process of cultural assimilation at the same time that it provides insight into discourse processes in a heterogeneous society.

NOTES

This chapter originally appeared in *Language and Social Identity,* edited by John Gumperz (Cambridge University Press, 1982). That version was itself a revision of an earlier version that appeared as "Indirectness in Discourse: Ethnicity as Conversational Style" in *Discourse Processes* 4(1981):3.221–38. I would like to repeat here the acknowledgements that appear there:

> I wish to thank directly Robin Tolmach Lakoff, who originally inspired and has continually enlightened my thinking about indirectness in discourse, and John Gumperz, who gave direction to the research reported here. In addition, I am grateful for comments on drafts of this and related work from Wallace Chafe, David Gordon, Dee Holisky, Dell Hymes, Kostas Kazazis, Bambi Schieffelin, and Cynthia Wallat. I want to thank all my informants, too numerous to name, but including Pam Fahlund, Jom Garofallou, Mathilde Paterakis, Georgette Stratos, and Theoni Velli-Spyropoulos; Daughters of Penelope District 5, New York; Pastor Peter Vourliotis, Faye Masterson, and Women's Ministries of the Greek Assembly of God, Oakland, California; Father Tom Paris, Mary Alevizos, and the Philoptochos Society of the Greek Orthodox Church of the Ascension, Oakland, California; John Kaiteris and the Hellenic American Neighborhood Action Committee, New York; and the Milvia Street Block Association, Berkeley, California. Finally, thanks to Angeliki Nikolopoulou and Aris Arapostathis for collaboration on Greek translations.

1. An earlier study (Tannen 1976) presented two different versions of this conversation with a rating-scale questionnaire. The two English versions differed in that one presented the husband's first response as "OK," while the other presented it as "yeah." The two Greek versions, administered in Athens, differed in that one presented the husband's first response as "OK" (*endaxi*), while the other presented it as the informal Greek "yes" (*ne*). Whereas I had expected the shift to "yes/yeah" to produce more choices of the direct interpretation among both Greeks and Americans, I found that the substitution of "yeah" for "OK" made no difference in American responses, while the substitution of "yes" (*ne*) for "OK" (*endaxi*) did yield fewer choices of the indirect interpretation by Greeks. In other words, "OK" and "yeah" turned out to be equivalents for English, whereas "OK" and "yes" did not turn out to be equivalents for Greeks. This difference

may be explained in part by the "yes/yeah" distinction in English, but I believe it is also attributable in part to the greater expectation among Greeks that objections will not be directly expressed, so one must attend to the indirect interpretation of "OK."

REFERENCES

Brown, Penelope, and Stephen Levinson. [1978]1987. Politeness: Some universals in language usage. Cambridge: Cambridge University Press.

Ervin-Tripp, Susan. 1976. Is Sybil there? The structure of some American English directives. Language in Society 5:1.25–66.

Goffman, Erving. 1959. The presentation of self in everyday life. New York: Doubleday.

Goody, Esther. 1978. Towards a theory of questions. Questions and politeness, ed. by Esther Goody, 17–43. Cambridge: Cambridge University Press.

Gumperz, John J., and Deborah Tannen. 1979. Individual and social differences in language use. Individual differences in language ability and language behavior, ed. by Charles Fillmore, Daniel Kempler, and William S.-Y. Wang, 305–24. New York: Academic Press.

Lakoff, Robin. 1973. The logic of politeness, or minding your p's and q's. Papers from the Ninth Regional Meeting of the Chicago Linguistics Society, 292–305.

Lakoff, Robin. 1975. Language and woman's place. New York: Harper and Row.

Lakoff, Robin Tolmach. 1979. Stylistic strategies within a grammar of style. Language, sex, and gender, ed. by Judith Orasanu, Mariam Slater, and Leonore Loeb Adler. Annals of the New York Academy of Science 327.53–78.

Scollon, Ron. 1985. The machine stops: Silence in the metaphor of malfunction. Perspectives on silence, ed. by Deborah Tannen and Muriel Saville-Troike, 21–30. Norwood, NJ: Ablex.

Seaman, P. David. 1972. Modern Greek and American English in contact. The Hague: Mouton.

Tannen, Deborah. 1976. An indirect/direct view of misunderstandings in conversation. Masters thesis, University of California, Berkeley.

Tannen, Deborah. 1981. New York Jewish conversational style. International Journal of the Sociology of Language 30.133–39.

Tannen, Deborah. 1984. Conversational style: Analyzing talk among friends. Norwood, NJ: Ablex.

Vassiliou, Vasso, Harry Triandis, George Vassiliou, and Howard McGuire. 1972. Interpersonal contact and stereotyping. The analysis of subjective culture, ed. by Harry Triandis, 89–115. New York: John Wiley.

Index

Lightning Source UK Ltd.
Milton Keynes UK
14 August 2009

142698UK00004B/1/A